Observing Children from Birth to 6

Also available from Bloomsbury

Reflective Teaching in Early Education Jennifer Colwell

Learning to Teach Young Children Anna Kirova, Larry Prochner and Christine Massing

Observing Children and Young People Carole Sharman, Wendy Cross and Diana Vennis

Observing Children from Birth to 6

A Practical Guide for Early Childhood Students and Practitioners

5th EDITION

Carole Sharman, Wendy Cross and Diana Vennis

BLOOMSBURY ACADEMIC
LONDON • NEW YORK • OXFORD • NEW DELHI • SYDNEY

BLOOMSBURY ACADEMIC
Bloomsbury Publishing Plc
50 Bedford Square, London, WC1B 3DP, UK
1385 Broadway, New York, NY 10018, USA
29 Earlsfort Terrace, Dublin 2, Ireland

BLOOMSBURY, BLOOMSBURY ACADEMIC and the Diana logo are trademarks of
Bloomsbury Publishing Plc

First published in Great Britain 1995
This edition published 2022

For legal purposes the Acknowledgements on p. xv constitute an extension
of this copyright page.

Cover design: Charlotte James
Cover image © lostinbids/ Getty Images

A catalogue record for this book is available from the British Library.

Library of Congress Cataloging-in-Publication Data

Names: Sharman, Carole, author. | Cross, Wendy, author. | Vennis, Diana, author.
Title: Observing children from birth to 6 : a practical guide for early childhood students
and practitioners / Carole Sharman, Wendy Cross, Diana Vennis.
Other titles: Observing children from birth to six
Description: 5th edition. | New York, NY : Bloomsbury Academic, 2022. |
Originally published under title: Observing children, 1995. |
Includes bibliographical references and index.
Identifiers: LCCN 2022003839 (print) | LCCN 2022003840 (ebook) |
ISBN 9781350135406 (hardback) | ISBN 9781350135390 (paperback) |
ISBN 9781350135420 (ePDF) | ISBN 9781350135413 (eBook)
Subjects: LCSH: Child psychology–Research–Methodology. |
Observation (Psychology–Methodology.
Classification: LCC BF722 .S47 2022 (print) | LCC BF722 (ebook) |
DDC 155.4—dc23/eng/20220214
LC record available at https://lccn.loc.gov/2022003839
LC ebook record available at https://lccn.loc.gov/2022003840

ISBN: HB: 978-1-3501-3540-6
       PB: 978-1-3501-3539-0
       ePDF: 978-1-3501-3542-0
       eBook: 978-1-3501-3541-3

Typeset by RefineCatch Limited, Bungay, Suffolk

To find out more about our authors and books visit www.bloomsbury.com
and sign up for our newsletters.

Contents

Figures

Contributors

Sarah Barton, BA – Social Studies Teacher Education, QTS Primary Education, MA – education, Professional Doctorate Student – Early Childhood Education, Portsmouth Research Portal contributor 2020. Sarah is Senior Lecturer and Programme Leader for the Early Years Initial Teacher Training Programme leading to Early Years Teacher Status (EYTS), Tutor on the Foundation Degree (EYCE) and the BA in Early Childhood Studies at the University of Portsmouth, UK. Sarah has been a consultant to the authors, advising on present practice in current University Early Years courses.

Wendy Cross, N.N.E.B, DPQS, Certificate of Education (FE), D32/D33 Assessor, D34 Internal Assessor, D35 External Assessor (City and Guilds). At the beginning of her career Wendy set up and owned a very successful nursery. After gaining her Certificate of Education she taught in Further Education where she was Course Leader for the Council for Awards in Care, Health and Education (CACHE) courses and an assessor and Verifier for National Vocational Qualifications (NVQ) level 2 and 3 in Early Years.

Julie Pickthall, BA – Early Childhood Studies, Certificate of Education (Early Years). Julie is the Early Years Practice Manager at Steady Steps Nursery and Pre-School, Rowner, Gosport, UK. The authors visited the nursery to discuss current trends in observations, current nursery practice, and the use of technology to record children's progress and liaise with parents and other professionals.

Anne Purdon, BA – History, MA – Early Childhood Studies. Anne is a Senior Lecturer in Early Years at Norland College, Bath, UK. She has contributed to the section on the ethical aspect of undertaking observations in Chapter 1. The authors discussed with Anne and a number of other staff at Norland College the impact of governmental changes in Early Years provision and practice.

Carole Sharman, SRN – General Nursing, Certificate of Education (Primary), Health Visitor, D32/D33 Assessor, D34 Internal Assessor (City and Guilds) began her career in the medical profession, working in hospitals and with children under 5 in the community. After retraining, she taught in an infant school and then in Further Education where she became Head of Department for Early Years and Special Educational Needs. After retiring she worked as a self-employed Consultant in Early Years.

Diana Vennis, Certificate in Education, (Early Years), D32/D33 Assessor, D34 Internal Assessor, D35 External Assessor (CACHE), Ofsted Nursery Inspector, Associate Inspector for Adult Learning, Early Years. After teaching in Nursery and Infant schools Diana worked in Further Education for twenty-five years where she was a lecturer and Course Supervisor for the Council for Awards in Care, Health and Education (CACHE), an Eternal Verifier for CACHE, a registered Ofsted Inspector for Early Years settings and an Associate Inspector for the Adult Learning Inspectorate for Early Years Courses.

Preface

This book is intended for use by anyone studying, or intending to work with children aged from birth to 6 years. The main aim is to enable practitioners to develop their experience of observing children so as to recognize their skills and abilities. Observing to identify any particular need is also essential in order to provide an environment where they can progress.

During most university foundation and degree courses covering Early Years Care and Education, students are given opportunities to develop differing observational techniques. This enables them to analytically reflect and to be critical of their findings in order to compare with recognized developmentalists, theorists, and behaviourists that they are researching and studying. While the move in schools is to follow the Early Adopter Framework for recording children's progress, this does require a deal of experience on the part of the teacher. Written evidence is enhanced by the teacher's knowledge of individual children in order to record progress. However students may find it easier to have some form of written evidence on which to base their reflections, assessment and planning. What, and how, children learn physically, mentally, socially, as well as intellectually, in the early years is known to have lifelong effects on their abilities to cope and progress.

This book aims to give students a focus on appropriate techniques and applications for different observation methods. It is not linked specifically to any course of study or area of work but, where practical, links are made to the Early Learning Goals for the Foundation Stage when discussing prime areas of development. By presenting evidence in the form of direct observation, for the workplace recording system or, when requested, to other professionals if a child needs to be referred, it will demonstrate a detailed knowledge of development and the principles underlying different methods of presenting the data. It should enable consideration of each child's strengths and possible weaknesses to make sure that they have been given every opportunity to show what they can do by reflecting on the method chosen and the result it gives.

How to use this book

This book is intended as a source of reference that can be dipped into when required. However if you are not familiar with formal observations, and many courses no longer require an observation file to be submitted, you might want to read through the book in the order that it is written. The chapters have been designed to lead you through the process, building on knowledge gained earlier.

Acknowledgements

The following people were willing to discuss how observations are utilized in their establishments to follow the Early Years Foundation Stage and assist planning.

Charles Beckerson, Headteacher, St. Bartholomew School.

Laura Burton, B.A. Early Years Specialist, Reception and year 1 Teacher, St. Bartholomew School.

Deborah Cross, Teaching Assistant, St. Bartholomew School.

Jo Henderson, Deputy Assistant Principal, Chichester College.

We would also like to thank Oliver (4), Dylan (10 months) and the children of Steady Steps nursery who appear in the book, and their parents for giving permission for them to be included.

Introduction

Watching children at play, resting, absorbed in an activity or roaming, alone or with others, can give us indications of how they are developing and starting to organize their thinking.

Children, especially those between birth and 6 years, learn best by what they gather through their senses. Using this information they can begin to test out ideas, a process known as experiential learning that involves making meaning from direct experience. As Aristotle said: 'For the things we have to learn before we can do them, we learn by doing them.'

The role of the observer is to try to understand what the child wants from an activity and, if necessary, provide appropriate opportunities for the practitioner to 'focus on supporting and extending children's learning in the moment' (Julian Grenier – DfE *Development Matters*, 2021).

We need to avoid falling into the trap though, that all play must have an intellectual outcome. If we limit outcomes in this way we miss the opportunity to discover what benefits the child is getting, that we had not thought of, including information from parents and others shared via online podcasts that could be influencing the play. This is one reason for carrying out observations without intervention, while supervising the children's safety.

The term 'Emotional Intelligence' was introduced by Daniel Goleman (*Working with Emotional Intelligence*, 1999), but the concept had been long understood. Children will learn best when they feel happy, supported and in control.

In *Development Matters* (2021, p. 5), the DfE (Department for Education) states, as one of the seven key features of effective practice, that: 'Babies, toddlers and young children thrive when they are loved and well cared for.'

The Early Years Foundation Stage Statutory Framework (DfE, 2017, p. 5) states: 'Children develop quickly in the early years and a child's experiences between birth and age five years have a major impact on their future life chances.'

DfE *Development Matters* (2021, p. 4) states: 'All children learn more in the period from birth to five years old than at any other time in their lives.' And 'When we succeed in giving every child the best start in their early years, we give them what they need today. We also set them up with every chance of success tomorrow'.

They therefore require rich opportunities to initiate ideas and activities.

Every child is unique and needs to be interested and motivated by what they are doing. They need to feel in control of their activities and to be able to try things out for themselves. Early Years practitioners will recognize that children will retain knowledge better if they have learned to solve problems, rather than been taught to memorize. If children are told something that they do not understand they may become anxious and frustrated, and they will certainly soon forget it. If we are able to observe how children have come to an answer, we are able to give more relevant support. This type of observation should be quick and easy, and most importantly, used for the benefit of the child. This is the reason why quite large sections of the book concentrate on how to utilize the observations that you have recorded. It focuses on the way that observations can be used to give a more complete picture of individual children's strengths, interests and possible developmental delay. These can then be used to plan activities for individual children or groups who have common needs and interests 'Observation planning is an essential activity in early years as it enhances practice and offers meaningful links between children's learning and development and the early years curriculum' (Palaiologou, 2016).

The need to plan for individual children is at the core of the EYFS (Early Years Foundation Stage) ethos, and this planning should follow careful observation of children's play to enable activities to be child-led and therefore more sustained. 'The child's experience must always be central to the thinking of every practitioner' (DfE *Development Matters*, 2021, p. 5).

> **Chapter 1** – 'Why Do Observations?' discusses why observation should be an integral part of everyday practice in order to collect information about individual children for assessment, and to reflect on their needs. It outlines the principles for obtaining reliable and accurate assessment, and considers ethical and confidentiality issues when undertaking observations. It summarizes the most common observational techniques and the pros and cons of each format when deciding the most appropriate method. It describes how they can be used to benefit the child and also enrich your own learning.

> **Chapter 2** – 'Observational Techniques' provides a step-by-step guide to presenting a formal written observation. This includes identifying the aim or purpose for the observation and the reasons for each of the

headings normally used, while recognizing that this formal type of observation is not usually employed unless undertaking research or when difficulties in any area have been identified. There are activities to help consolidate the learning and encourage the reader to reflect on the findings. Scenarios that may occur naturally are described, but specific observations with predetermined aims/focuses are also included. These may be required where a problem is suspected or where naturally occurring evidence has not been possible.

Chapter 3 – 'A Guide to Presenting and Experimenting with Observational Techniques' demonstrates ways to record in different formats and to consider the strengths and weaknesses of each method. It covers diagrammatic, sampling, written, checklist and online learning journals. The examples given have mostly been undertaken because a specific concern has been raised and observation is required to provide clear evidence.

Chapter 4 – 'Extending and Utilizing Your Observations' encourages the reader to consider and recognize the importance of observations when planning for the children in your care. It also recognizes that working with parents, and understanding the roles and responsibilities of other professionals, is an important tool when considering how to meet individual children's needs.

Observations may also be required to assist when completing the two-year progress check and EYFS profile when children move from reception to key stage one. This is important if the Early Years staff have not seen a skill demonstrated during normal day-to-day activities.

Chapter 5 – 'Providing Activities to Support Planning within Early Years Environments' encourages the reader to be aware and appreciate the importance of a well-planned environment that allows children to make new discoveries. To have an awareness of what is required in order to plan for short, medium and long-term goals for advancing children's learning. To understand the ways that materials can be utilized that foster an interest in the environment and the importance of conservation of the earth's resources. The activities suggest ways to provide an enabling environment that will encourage children to take charge of their learning and move forward in their development.

'A well planned learning environment, indoors and outside, is an important aspect of pedagogy' (DfE *Development Matters*, 2021, p. 6).

Chapter 6 – 'Outline of Development from Birth to 6 Years' provides a summary of the main focus points of children's development from birth to 6 years, which includes the age range birth to 5 years covered by the Early Years Foundation Stage.

The underlying theories of development, and the theorists and behaviourists who support them, are described. Student activities are used to encourage reflection, reinforce what has been learnt, and encourage ways to support development.

The aim of this book is to make you aware of the value of carrying out observations, and the ways that they can be used for the benefit of the children in your care. How observing what children are doing naturally can lead to planning an environment that is rich in opportunity for unique development.

Note: Throughout the book there are some references taken from much earlier publications in order to illustrate a point. They may reflect changing times and theories but also allow the reader to reflect on how some fundamental ideas have remained constant.

Why do Observations?

-
-
-

Government guidelines and many textbooks linked to Early Years Degrees or vocational courses describe the importance of undertaking observations, and using them to reflect on what they are telling us about how a child is developing and learning. They are an invaluable tool when planning ways to move a child forward and enabling them to reach their full potential.

Vicky Cortvriend and Iain Macleod-Brudenell support the above statement.

'Observation of children should be used to inform and strengthen our support for all aspects of child development in every context' and 'Extending skills for the complex process of observing children helps develop skills in reflection. In addition, it will enable you to achieve the analytical and reflective skills required for work at degree level' (Macleod-Brudenell et al., 2008).

The EYFS framework *Early Adopter Handbook* (DfE, 2020) comments: 'Teachers' judgements will largely be based on their observations during day-to-day activity in the classroom. They should draw on this knowledge and their own expert professional judgement to make an accurate summative assessment at the end of the year.'

Below is a list of some of the comments made by practitioners and parents about the children in their care:

'I wonder why he did that?' (Child has thrown water all over the floor.)

'She shows little understanding of what I would like her to do.' (Child does not comprehend a simple task involving cutting out shapes for pattern-building activity.)

'Finds it difficult to share toys with the other children.'

'The outbursts of temper seem to be getting worse . . . when will they stop?' (Child becomes very emotional when attempting difficult tasks.)

Activity 1

Reflect on the answers to the following questions:

What could be the reason for the behaviours described?

What suggestions might you make to ease the situation?

Is the behaviour something to worry about?

What action would you take in short/long term planning?

When reflecting on these questions would it have been easier if we had known how old the child was, and what was expected behaviour for that age? Also would it be easier if we had actually observed the behaviour and in what situation it was taking place?

This chapter aims to give you the tools to make best use of observations and what they can tell us, and in Chapter 6 expected parameters of development are discussed.

Why do we observe children?

One of the main reasons we observe and assess is to find out if children are following the general pathway of development for their age. Observation is an important tool for you to use to reflect on what you have seen and make comparisons theoretical perspectives. In the Early Years Foundation Stage (further referred to as EYFS), it is stated that 'observation is the most reliable way of building up an accurate picture of the child's development and learning – observational assessment is key to understanding what children really know and understand, then put this knowledge into action'. EYFS principles for obtaining reliable and accurate assessment are regarded as essential in order to give children the best opportunity to demonstrate their learning and development skills. The principles state that: 'Responsible pedagogy must be in place so that the provision enables each child to demonstrate their learning and development fully.

Embedded learning is identified by assessing what a child can do consistently and independently in a range of everyday situations. An effective assessment presents a holistic view of a child's learning and development' (*EYFS Profile Handbook*, section 2.2, 2014).

All children will develop at their own rate. There are genetic and environmental influences that can affect the rate at which they progress, but broadly they will follow the same sequence.

Many researchers have studied the progression of children's development in a variety of areas, and their results are available to you in the textbooks, online and other media so that you can research and refer to them in your own studies. These may include very well recognized theorists like Piaget, Bowlby and Vygotsky, but all researchers are likely to use observations to gain firsthand information about children's development. For instance, Early Years consultant Sandy Green (2002) states: 'Researchers throughout the health and social care sector may use observations as primary research to gain information within child and young adult settings.'

When observing children, students should be as unobtrusive as possible so as not to disrupt or alter behaviour. They should also be fully aware of the ethical and confidentiality aspects of undertaking observations.

There are many issues to consider when observing children, but one of the most important is the ethical aspect. This must be considered as we know that young children may be more vulnerable and at risk from adults (Palaiologou, 2016). This is supported by the Code of Ethics outlined in Early Education (2020) that places the utmost importance on the protection and wellbeing of children and families. To maintain this protection anybody wishing to work with children is required to have a DBS (Disclosure and Barring Service) formally known as the CRB (Criminal Records Bureau).

Early Years Practitioners (EYPs) should not only gain consent from the parents or carers to carry out an observation, but also gain assent from the children themselves (Papatheodrou, Luff and Gill, 2011). Children can communicate their discomfort through non-verbal language such as crying or gestures from a very young age. UNICEF (1989) supports this by stressing the importance of ensuring the 'best interests of the child'. Both parents and child should also be given the option to refuse to allow an observation at any time.

Written consent is needed from parents or carers before observing, taking photographs or making records, and most Early Years settings have a blanket cover letter to give this consent while the child is at the setting. This should ensure that all parties are fully aware of the process (DfE, 2017). However, it is vital that this letter is kept up to date (Brodie, 2013) and that checks are made to make sure that the person signing the document actually has the authority to give consent. In order to gain informed consent, EYP should provide clear information, and to avoid deception the observation should provide a specific focus that is clear and transparent for the parent or carer.

Ethical issues are not just about consent but also about open dialogue enabling all participants in the process to be involved (Palaiologou, 2012). Providing details about the purpose of the observation and the use and storage of the records enables the consent to be informed consent.

The observation method used must be appropriate for the child being observed, but ethically children should also be observed using a variety of methods, and in a range of contexts, in order to give them the best opportunity to demonstrate their strengths. 'Written observations need to be factual, objective and avoid making any assumptions or comparisons with other children, as each child will develop at their own rates and in their own ways' (British Association for Early Childhood Education, 2012).

The need for confidentiality should also be addressed when using observations as a tool for assessment. EYP should understand the need for children's privacy to ensure they are protected (UNICEF, 1989; DfE, 2017). If a student on placement is undertaking the observation as part of the study programme in order to reflect on outcomes, then only the age and type of setting are required. If the observation is to be used to enhance the child profile in the setting, then obviously the child's name will be required. These observations would be governed by the *Data Protection Act 2018* and would need to be processed confidentially and stored safely. The EYFS (DfE, 2017) also explains that parents should be provided with access to information about their child, and that it can only be shared with outside agencies with written parental permission. However, child protection issues will always supersede the need for confidentiality.

As well as using observations to discover how children are developing and behaving, we can also utilize them in order to plan play areas that enable children to explore freely and express their unique personalities. By observing children as they move around an area, watching how they interact with their surroundings and other children, we can reflect on what we might provide in order to help them consolidate a skill or move forward.

Having decided that observation is a tool that will help you with understanding how children develop, and thus benefit your knowledge and also benefit the children, we need to consider the best way to carry out the observations and record the results.

It is suggested in the EYFS handbook that 'some observations will be planned but some may be a spontaneous capture of an important moment'. These 'in the moment' observations are invaluable when completing child profiles and will also be useful for reflection, but the following section discusses the different methods that can be used when we seek to understand where a child is in their development, and plan for the observation. During the time that students are undertaking programmes of studies in Early Years there is a wonderful opportunity to undertake more formal observations, to enable reflection and reference to theorists in order to consolidate knowledge of child development.

Before proceeding it is important to consider a couple of points:

1 An observation is like a camera shot, and although it is said that the camera does not lie, it may distort. We should not make any judgments about children based upon a single observation. We may have been alerted to a possible problem but would need to follow it up in order to reach an informed conclusion after reflection and discussion.

2 The very fact that we are carrying out an observation can make a difference to the way that children behave. They may become inhibited or embarrassed, or may play to the audience. For example, if children are not used to having a photo taken to record what they are doing, they will often want to 'pose'. You may want to take lots of pretend photos so that the children see it as a normal part of the routine and continue with their activity.

If you remember these points, they should help you to make the best use of your observations, and also to decide which might be the best method to use in order to record them for reflecting on the child's progress.

Researchers may use digital equipment to record children's behaviour in order that they can play it back on several occasions to see responses in detail; this is particularly useful when observing babies' actions. You may be able to use digital equipment with parental permission, but we are concentrating on the more usual methods of written evidence. The method you choose will normally be dependent upon the timescale and what you are hoping to discover.

In the following pages we discuss:

- Observation styles and methods.
- Children's needs and experiences.
- Skills you may observe.

Observation methods

Observations can be carried out in many formats, and the examples shown here demonstrate examples of how they may be recorded. In following chapters, we will be discussing all the methods you might employ, their different formats and the exact way to set out observations to enable their optimum use for assessment purposes.

1. Narrative/free description

This involves observing a child or group of children and noting down what you see. If planned, you need to sit quietly and try to draw as little attention to yourself as possible, remembering that your interaction with the children can affect their behaviour.

Narrative observations usually cover a short period of time. They should be written in the present tense as they are recording actions and narratives as they occur. Although you may need to set the scene by initially describing what is happening around you, you need to remember that your main focus is the child you are observing. In practice, many childcare settings are using Post-it notes or iPads to record a series of short narratives to build up a profile of a child's progress. However, if you are completing observations as part of a course of study, and in order to use them for the purpose of reflection, it is probably more beneficial to use the longer form.

The following examples demonstrate the differences.

Observation/example 1, longer form

Setting: Home corner in reception class

Jayden and Liam sit down at the table and start to arrange the plates and cups that have been left out. Jayden says, 'We need to have knives and forks.' Liam remains seated so Jayden gets up and opens the drawer to take out cutlery.

Liam goes over to the basket containing plastic food items. He chooses a pizza and puts it into the oven. A moment later he takes it out and says 'hot'. He puts the pizza onto the table and sits down.

Mylie wheels her pushchair into the area and collects a doll from the cot. She attempts to sit down at the table, but Jayden calls out: 'No, we are having dinner.' Mylie moves away.

Jayden brings over the cutlery and sits down. The boys pretend to eat.

Both boys get up and move out of the area.

EYP reminds to tidy up if they have finished.

Observation/example 2, Post-it notes

Jayden in home corner

Talks to Liam.
Recognizes needs cutlery on table.
Able to maintain role-play.
Not willing to include Mylie in role-play.
Needs reminder to clear up.

Liam in home corner

Shows understanding that pizza needs to go in oven and get hot.
Able to sustain role-play.
Little language used.
Needs reminder to tidy up.

Mylie in home corner

Mylie in home corner to collect doll for her pushchair.
Attempts to sit with Liam at the table.
Told 'no' by Jayden and moves away.

Activity 2

Compare and contrast the difference in the evidence gathered when using the longer form of the written/narrative and the Post-it note format.

This type of observation is most often used to record information on children's EYFS profile. They are not planned but record daily activities as they occur.

2. Checklists/pre-coded categories

Checklists can be used to record the activities of a single child or a group of children. Unlike the written/narrative observation that only requires you to record behaviours occurring naturally, a checklist needs to be prepared in advance. This form of observation will normally have an aim where you identify the presence or absence of predetermined behaviours, skills etc. Checklists are regularly used in Early Years establishments to record children's progress. It is important for the teacher or EYP to be aware of the needs of the individual child so that programmes can be developed that will benefit their progress.

Children have a lot of freedom to decide their own learning activities, so it is essential to keep records of their achievements. It is important to note here that we are recording a child's achievements, not their failure to do something. Of course, we may identify a need while we are doing so.

3. Time sampling/structured description

As the name suggests, this form of recording consists of a series of written records observed at intervals throughout a period of time. The length of time between the observations, and the period of time you observe for, will depend on the overall timescale for the completed record. This will normally be decided by the reason you have identified for carrying out the observation in the first place. For example, if you wanted to discover whether a child is able to concentrate for the duration of story time, you might decide to observe that child every minute and record what they are doing. However in a busy setting it can be difficult to remember to keep your attention on one child.

If a child was showing aggressive behaviour or appeared not to mix with the other children, you might want to observe them for a morning or even a whole day. It would be impractical to observe at minute intervals so you might choose to make the interval twenty minutes or half an hour.

4. Tracking/structured description

A tracking observation involves following a child for a period of time to discover where they go and what they do. This could be recorded as a written observation, but an alternative is to show the result in the form of a diagram or photograph of the area where the child will be working in advance. This might be the nursery, classroom or outdoor play area. The most obvious use would be to record the activities a child chooses, how long they spend in each area or the number of social contacts they may have. It would enable you to see if they stay with one activity or move from one to another, and the reasons for this movement. This would give useful information for future planning of the environment.

5. Pie and bar charts

Pie and bar charts are a useful pictorial way of recording the results of an observation of a group of children. For instance, you might want to discover how many children in the group can manage a physical skill like catching a ball. One way of doing this would be to set up an activity where you throw a ball to the child from a distance of a metre. Your record would show how many children were able to catch the ball three times out of three; two times out of three; once out of three; or not at all. If your results showed that the children had some difficulty with this, you might introduce some activities that give practice in the skill and then repeat the observation to see if there had been improvement.

These methods have many uses for collecting information about the children, but they can also be used to give objective evidence about the equipment used in the nursery and classroom. You can observe areas in the setting and note how many times an activity is freely chosen. This could give an opportunity in the future – or where to position yourself to give added interest. Reflecting on how the classroom is set out, and possible changes, could encourage more freedom of movement and better use of resources.

Figures 1.1 and 1.2 demonstrate how the charts may look.

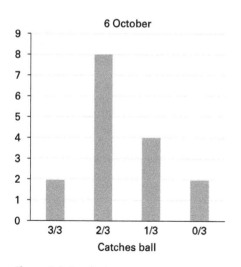 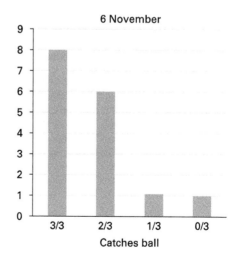

Figure 1.1 Bar chart.

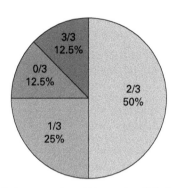

Before practice 50% caught 2/3 balls

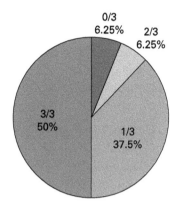

After practice 50% caught 3/3 balls

Figure 1.2 Pie chart.

6. Longitudinal/child profile

In practice, longitudinal observations are often undertaken when a child has a special need that may be affecting development, and a record over time is used to assess progress. However, many courses of study require students to complete a child profile. This can provide a record of expected development, which will reinforce the knowledge gained from books. The usual period of time for this method of observation is six months to a year. The following observation covers the progress of a child from nine weeks to eight months. Physical and social development is very discernable during this time and is the primary focus of the observation.

Observation 1 (nine weeks)

When prone, Dylan is able to lift his head for approximately seven seconds in response to a rattle being shaken above his head. This appears to take a lot of effort as Dylan quickly tires after the play session. When lifted up by his father, he responds to the smile by smiling.

Observation 2 (eleven weeks)

Dylan looks in the direction of the speaker when music is being played. He shows his excitement by kicking his legs and making a gurgling sound.

Dylan concentrates on faces for longer. He mimics smiles frequently, especially with familiar adults.

Dylan maintains eye contact when spoken to and demonstrates early speech sounds by babbling and gurgling.

Observation 3 (twelve weeks)

Dylan enjoys being held under the arms in a sitting position. He is able to hold his head in an upright position for up to a minute before tiring. When sat up he is able to follow an object with his eyes and turn his head.

Dylan is moving his limbs more purposefully. He reaches for objects but eye/hand coordination is not yet developed enough for him to successfully grasp them. He enjoys reaching for the toy that sings in response to being touched.

Observation 4 (thirteen weeks)

Dylan enjoys looking at himself in a mirror and smiles after studying his reflection for a few seconds. He now smiles at less familiar adults and children who smile at him.

Dylan has begun to explore more sensory objects. He enjoys the sound of the crackling wet wipes wrapper during nappy changing and likes to play with the 'feely' toys. He enjoys reaching for the toy that sings in response to being touched and exploring different sounds.

Observation 5 (four months)

Dylan is now very responsive to people and babbles, mimics and interacts with his carers. He is more expressive and has begun laughing when being played with. He now anticipates when something familiar is going to happen, for example when singing 'Round and Round the Garden' he begins to smile before laughing at 'Tickly under there....'.

Dylan holds himself in a seated position when supported. He can now grasp toys and brings them to his mouth to explore. He is showing signs of teething.

When prone, Dylan pushes up onto his elbows, but he seems to like being on his tummy less. He is attempting to reach out for toys and is often successful. He appears to favour noisy toys and teethers.

Observation 6 (five months)

Dylan now loves to blow raspberries, which he demonstrates during playtime and in his cot before falling asleep. He is responding to songs by smiling and becoming more animated. He has just begun making a roaring sound as he experiments with his voice.

Dylan is now sitting independently for up to a minute before needing support or becoming wobbly. He seems to prefer sitting upright, rather than on his front, and enjoys shaking his rattles.

Observation 7 (six months)

Dylan is very giggly. He understands when someone is being humorous and laughs in response, for example when someone plays 'Boo' or tickles him.

He is now showing signs of shyness with strangers, and favours people he recognizes. When held he tends to grab at people's faces as he explores.

Dylan has started shouting and his babbles are sounding more like words. He is very responsive to his name and will turn to face the speaker.

He can support himself while standing by holding onto something such as a chair or coffee table.

Observation 8 (seven months)

Dylan can now sit and play independently. He is aware when people come and go and will sometimes cry when they leave. He gets very excited when he sees family, wriggling his whole body and smiling. He is increasingly vocal and has begun to say 'Mumma'.

Dylan is now attempting to crawl. He moves from sitting to all fours and rocks back and forth, extending his legs outwards so he is in a planking position.

Observation 9 (eight months)

Dylan can say 'Mumma', 'Dadda', 'Indie' (family dog) and 'Yeah'.

He now definitely recognizes strangers as being different from family and will bury his head to 'hide' from them.

Dylan is crawling very fast, using a commando style. He pulls to stand and is beginning to cruise along the furniture.

He claps and waves and will start clapping when he hears 'If you're happy and you know it'. He understands the instructions 'bang', 'splash', arms up', 'clap', 'wave' and 'come here'.

This method of observation should help you gain a broader knowledge and understanding of development at this early stage, and also keep the practitioner informed as to progress or any development delays in future observations to alert you if you encounter any delays in future observations.

Activity 3

Read through the observation following Dylan's progress and answer the following:

Is Dylan following the expected pattern of development?

Are any areas of development giving cause for concern?

Is he using language in a meaningful way?

Give reasons for your answers.

You have now had the opportunity to consider the ways that observations can be written, and the most common observation formats. Table 1.1 discusses their pros and cons before deciding on which to use.

Understanding children's needs and experiences

One of the reasons identified for carrying out observations was 'to meet the needs of children in our care'. Children are all unique, and to be aware of their qualities we need to:

- Take an interest in what they are doing.
- Listen to what they are saying.
- Learn by reflecting on what they are telling us.

Children may communicate their needs in a variety of individual ways. Older children may be able to tell you what they want but could signal their need for support by the way they are behaving. Younger children usually demonstrate their needs using more primitive methods. For instance, one child may scream for attention while another may bite a child or adult to express their frustrations. Both these behaviours are anti-social, but we might understand the reasons if we observe why the behaviour is occurring.

Observation

Adam (20 months) is playing with a ball in the garden. He throws it into the air and then tries to kick it. He moves the ball by walking into it. When it rolls under a chair he laughs and shouts 'goal'.

Two older children (3 and 4 years old) come out of the house to watch. When the ball comes near to one he picks it up and they start to throw it to each other.

Adam stands and watches, waiting for his turn, but they do not include him in the game. The ball rolls towards Adam and he picks it up and hugs it to himself.

The 4-year-old walks over and takes it out of Adam's hands, then kicks it to the other child.

Adam tries to get the ball back, but the 3-year-old laughs, picks it up and holds it above her head. As she lowers her arms, Adam runs over and bites her hand. She screams and the adults run out to see what has happened.

Adam just stands, looking bewildered.

If we take this example of biting, the observation could help to sort out the problem and why it occurred. Adam really would have benefitted if the adults had been watching. They may have intervened before the incident ended with a bite. As he develops, Adam will recognize that there are other strategies for dealing with the situation.

Another example of the benefit of observation is to demonstrate a child's significant achievements. Children always want you to see what they can see. If you watch with them, experiences can be shared together. A child's excitement is intense when they shout, 'look at me!' If you observe children while they are working instead of just admiring the end product you may be surprised at their abilities.

For example, a child presents a soggy brown painting to be put in the drying rack. The Early Years Practitioner comments, 'I hope it will dry by going home time.'

When presented with the painting, the mother says, 'Very nice dear, what else have you done this morning?'

The following observation demonstrates what the picture represents and just how much learning the child has demonstrated.

Observation

Dionne (4 years, 1 month) puts on an apron and walks over to the painting table. She takes a brush from the brown paint pot and draws a circle. She puts two blobs of paint in the circle and returns brush to pot. She takes the blue brush and draws a body and legs, then says 'Grandma'.

She uses the red brush to paint a curved line at the top of the paper, and then puts a green line below it. She smiles and says, 'rainbow'. She stands back for a moment, then uses the yellow brush to paint a sun next to the rainbow. 'Now we need rain.' She paints blobs of brown paint onto the picture.

'It's raining very hard - here's a puddle.' She begins to paint lines of brown all over the picture. 'It's pouring - grandma is getting very wet!'

Dionne stands back and looks at the brown picture. 'I've finished.'

Dionne has demonstrated representation by a number of differing pictures that was not obvious in the end result when the rain covered them. She understood the connection between sun and rain in order to produce a rainbow. She produced a good representation of a person. It is so beneficial for a child if you spend time observing and listening while they are engaged in an activity rather than relying on the end product to assess their skills.

Children are very proud of their achievements, but you need to remember that their ability to do something will often depend on the amount of practice they have had. You should not be tempted to make a judgment from a single observation of a child or question their level of development. You must reflect on their past experience and environment before making any evaluations.

Children need adults to notice their achievements and provide an environment to support their further development. Observing a child's progress and assessing how to provide for their needs in all areas can help them reach their full potential.

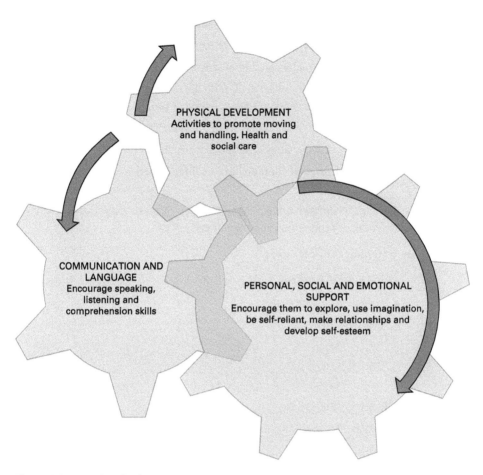

Figure 1.3 Promoting development.

Figure 1.3 gives some suggestions for ways that adults can promote development. Chapter 5, 'Providing Activities to Support Planning within Early Years Environments', covers in detail activities you can provide to enable children to make the best choices to further their development. You will notice that the areas are linked together, as it is inevitable that while you are providing for one you will also be covering others. Any activity could include language and hopefully also build self-esteem.

You have now looked at various observation methods, thought about children's needs and considered some of the skills you may require to encourage and develop children's progress.

These are some of the benefits you can learn by observing children:

- Discover how they approach problems and how they attempt to solve them.

- See how they make use of space and facilities.
- What level they have reached in their development.
- Have a better understanding of why a child may have done something.
- Reinforces our knowledge of child development and allows us to reflect upon our work practice with other professionals.
- Helps us to try to see things from the child's point of view
- Enables adults to study children in a structured format.
- You can learn that children have exciting experiences outside of the setting.
- Helps to support, underpin and plan activities, to support their early learning, progression and transitions.

By watching children, we:

- Evaluate their needs.
- Extend their experiences.
- Facilitate their learning.

Table 1.1 Comparison of observation types

Methods of observational techniques	Description	Usefulness	Pros	Cons
Narrative/Free description	Running records. Detailed account. Written description. Anecdotal. Seeing and hearing over a long period of time.	Recording children's behaviour – making lengthy notes during observation. Can use a video recording. Can be planned.	Can contain much information. Can contain unexpected/ spontaneous behaviour and activities. Close attention given to one child.	The recording often relies on the memory of the observer. Can take a considerable amount of time to record. Can impact the staff ratio rates, as observer is out of circulation.
Checklists	Collecting factual information. Focussing on observational behaviour/actions.	Monitor normal development stages – using development checklists or Portage or baseline tests. Observer can use their own checklist.	Gives an overview of a child or children's developmental stages. A checklist can be used again.	The focus is usually on developmental progress in a child or children.
Time Sampling/ Event Sampling	A certain activity, behaviour or event is the main focus. Short observations over time. Keep to a time schedule. Recognizing that children's behaviour may change and need closer monitoring.	A time schedule of undertaking observation – e.g. every 20 minutes observe – record for 2 to 3 minutes. Detection of a child's recurring or specific behaviour.	A complete and constant recording – it is a precise method of collecting data. It can be a brief record of a child's behaviour over time.	An explanation is not offered as to why the behaviour occurred. It can be difficult to use in a free flowing situation.

Table 1.1 (Continued)

Methods of observational techniques	Description	Usefulness	Pros	Cons
Tracking	A diagram or photograph of the area where children are being observed must be used. It is helpful to include a short-written engagement by the child in each area.	Used to find out how children make use of resources and space. You can focus on one child or several children, showing movements by direction arrows or in different colours.	Indicates visually the children's choices of equipment/activities and their movements. Gives staff a good idea of children's interest in various activities and equipment.	If activities cover several areas/rooms, then more than one observer may be required to watch free play. This way of observing has limited use.
Snapshot – wow moments – Post-its	A written sentence or two on a Post-it. Maybe taking a photograph.	Often catches one moment in a child's development. A Post-it helps to identify a child's development when used in sequence.	Short write-up by observer. A special unique moment is captured.	A good knowledge of child development is necessary in order to choose the best/right moment to write or take a photograph.
Online Learning Journal Audio/Visual recordings Child profiles/longitudinal	Conversation of a child or children by the use of mobile phones, iPad and audio-visual recorders. Use of detailed written evidence and pictorial evidence producing a complete journal of a child's learning. The majority of assessment happens in the moment.	Early Years Practitioners, parents and children contribute to learning journals. Positive outcomes are emphasized. Opportunity to easily review a child's progress.	This type of media enables observers to share observations and reflect on them with other members of staff and parents. Helps with a child's formative assessment record. Sharing information with parents is straightforward. Learning journals should be for significant moments – something new, something of importance that over time tells the story of a child's progress.	Analysis of video recordings can be complicated. It can take time to add photographs and written narrative to a child's learning journal.

Observational Techniques

A step-by-step guide: presenting a formal observation

-
-
-

Types of observational techniques

We will begin by looking in detail at how to organize and present an observation using the written/narrative format. To assist you through the stages that follow, the first example determines how a completed observation might look, with explanation for the headings used. The headings in bold type will actually always remain the same whichever format you use. An explanation for each heading is given in italic type.

Remember, observation is just the formal term for watching, noticing, noting and listening to children. It puts children at the centre of our practice, and allows us to see them as individuals, and then plan how to provide an environment that encourages progression.

In this instance the activity selected has been child originated, but for study purposes you may decide to undertake a formal observation where you organize a particular activity in order to assess a specific area of development. The format used here covers the areas normally required to set the observation in context, but your place of study may have an online recording programme specific to the setting for assessment and recording with the EYFS.

Observation

Date: 18 September 2018

There are two reasons for recording the date: (1) you may wish to repeat an observation at a later date in order to compare a child's ability with their previous performance; (2) it will enable you to work out the exact age of the child so that you can evaluate your results against the expected developmental stage.

Time commenced: 10.20 am   **Time completed:** 10.30 am

This allows you to comment more easily on the length of time a child spent on an activity.

Number of adults: 1   **Number of children:** 4

Although you may have decided to observe one child, it is useful to record the number of children in the group, as this may have an influence on the behaviour.

Name of child: Anna

It is only necessary to record the first name so that the record remains confidential if you are using the observation for study purposes.

Age: 3 years 10 months

You will need to know the child's date of birth to work this out. It is important to record the exact age in years and months in order to make a link with a relevant developmental stage.

Setting: The creative area of a nursery school. The children have a free choice of materials, but an Early Years Practitioner (EYP) is available to offer advice if required.

It is not necessary to identify the place by name in order to maintain confidentiality, but it is useful to record the general background to the observation. It is also important to record if an adult is involved as this is likely to affect the way the children behave.

Aim/focus/purpose: To observe a child who is nearly 4 years old during a creative session in order to identify fine motor skills and problem-solving ability.

The aim of an observation should set out the broad areas of development that you wish to find out. The terminology aim/focus/purpose may differ in different establishments but just means the reason why you are carrying out the observation and what you want to find out.

Record of observation

Anna puts on an apron and approaches the table, picks up a circular box, turns it over, then puts it back down. Walks round to other side of table, selects a cereal packet and returns to her original place. Looks at the adult and smiles.

'Have you decided what you want to make?' asks the EYP.

Anna looks at display on wall and says, 'a rocket'. She picks up silver foil and carefully tears it in half. With well-developed pincer grasp, she picks up glue spreader and dips it into glue pot. The EYP moves the pot closer to Anna as glue is dripping over table. Anna uses glue on spreader to smear over box, and then refills spreader.

Concentrating very hard, she uses spreader to cover the whole side. Smiles as she continues to make patterns in the glue.

Anna picks up silver paper with left hand and leans over to put more glue on spreader. She holds the paper in the palm of her hand and covers it with glue.

Anna places glue-covered silver paper onto the box. Her fingers stick to paper, which lifts off as she attempts to fix it to the box, but she perseveres.

Anna selects a cardboard tube. She pushes it against the box and holds it in position, but when she moves her hand the tube falls off. She picks up spreader and puts glue around the end then pushes it down on the box again. As she lets go, it falls over.

The EYP picks up another piece of cardboard tube. 'Shall I show you how you might fix it?'

Anna nods and watches as she makes a cut about two cm. long down the side.

'Can you make some more cuts around the edge?'

The EYP passes scissors to Anna who manages to put her fingers in them correctly and, holding the tube close to her body, she makes a short cut. She pulls scissors out and attempts a second incision. The scissors come together at an angle but do not cut. Anna begins to look anxious. EYP comes round the table and puts her hand over the scissors to guide them. Together they make several more cuts. Anna spreads more glue onto the end of the tube and pushes it down onto the box. When it stays in position she smiles. EYP praises for 'trying hard'. Anna looks very pleased, then goes to wash hands.

The record should be written as it happens whenever possible. You should record everything the child does but remember what your main focus was. In this instance other conversations and interactions took place but the aim was to discover Anna's fine manipulative skills and ability to problem solve.

Assessment of observation

Anna decided what she wanted to make before she started the model by observing what was on the wall frieze in the creative area. She was able to use the glue spreader and enjoyed putting lots of glue over the box. She used more than was necessary to stick the paper to it and spent some time making patterns, which she appeared to enjoy. Anna had some difficulty using the scissors, but she held them correctly. She was not yet able to work out how to fix the cardboard tube to the box but managed to complete her rocket with the assistance of the EYP, using scaffolding to guide her hand.

The conclusion should summarize what you observed and match it to what you hoped to find out.

Reflection/analysis

In Development Matters (DfE, 2018), for the 3- to 4-year-old it states that children 'Develop their own ideas and then decide which materials to use to express them' and 'Join different materials and explore different textures'. Anna is not quite 4 years old. She was able to name what she planned to do and to choose the materials she needed. With a little help she was able to join the materials and complete the task. Anna appears to be operating well within the expected outcomes for physical development and some aspects of 'children's thinking and discussion' within communication and language.

The reflection/analysis should compare your findings with what you expect children to be able to do at that age. You should use a recognized source in order to make your comparison. Examples could be in the milestones in Chapter 6 of this text, or from the chapter in Development Matters, 'Expressive Arts and Design'. Where possible you should also use current research or theorists.

Forward planning

Continue to offer opportunities for planning her own activities. Encourage activities that will help to strengthen finger muscles (fine motor skills) e.g. drawing, construction toys and using a wide range of tools and equipment.

Forward planning should consider activities and support that will assist the child to gain confidence and move forward in their development.

One of the main uses for your observation is to enable you to plan activities that will help children perfect their skills and move forward. By observing and reflecting on what the child is doing you can organize suitable activities. This is backed up by the research of Lev Vygotsky, who concluded that children could learn more by the right amount of adult intervention. He used the term 'Zone of Proximal Development' to explain the range of potential for learning each person has compared with the learning that actually takes place in their environment.

Zone of Proximal Development: the distance between the actual development level as determined by independent problem solving and the level of potential development as determined through problem solving under adult guidance or in collaboration with more capable peers. *(Vygotsky, 1978)*

This is further endorsed by the work of Piaget, as noted by McLeod (2018). According to Piaget (Inhelder & Piaget, 1958), assimilation and accommodation require an active learner, not a passive one, because problem-solving skills cannot be taught, they must be discovered. Within the classroom, learning should be student-centred and accomplished through active discovery learning. The role of the teacher is to facilitate learning, rather than direct tuition.

Now that you have seen how a completed observation is set out you should be ready to try the skill for yourself. The following sections have been arranged so that you can work through the activities and build on your knowledge.

Tips for recording your observations

It is not easy to record what is taking place as you are trying to watch everything that is happening around you. While you are recording you may miss an important interaction.

If you record and discuss the observation while it is fresh in your mind you will often be able to visualize the situation again and know what and why you have recoded this information. Another way to make your recording easier is to identify clearly the reason why you are observing the child and what you hope to find out. This will give you your aim/focus.

Activity 1

Following is a fifteen-minute observation of two 4-year-old boys during free play outside. There are other children present, and they have access to several large objects.

Study the observation and reflect on what it tells you about their development. Suggestions are given at the end.

Observation

The children are in the outside area during a period of free play. Mason looks round then starts to collect planks of wood, which he puts in a pile on the grass. He stands observing what else is available and spots two large drums that have been used to coil wire. He starts to roll one over towards the wood. Declan collects another one and also rolls it towards the wood. Mason looks round and says, 'No, put it over the other side.' 'What shall we build?' asks Declan. Mason does not answer and just continues to walk around looking at the equipment.

Mason picks up a plank of wood and rests it against the drum. Declan collects another plank and stands looking at the drum. Mason pulls the second drum closer and says, 'put the drum on top'. He spots some plastic crates and uses them to extend the structure. Both boys collect more planks and build a longer run over the crates by carefully balancing various lengths of wood.

Mason picks up a long plank of wood that is resting against the wall and tries to manoeuvre it vertically towards other children. The plank falls forward and teacher reminds him to 'be careful near your friends'.

Mason picks up a stack of plastic cones and struggles to pull them apart. He perseveres and stands deciding what to do with them. He approaches a drum to put one on top, but another child has walked up the plank and is standing on it. Mason tries to move him and ends up pushing him off. Teacher intervenes to check child is unhurt, and reminds Mason, 'it is not good to hurt our friend'. The boys resume finishing the walkway by adding more planks to the structure in order to join up the drums and crates. Mason turns to Declan and says, 'let's test it'.

Carefully they balance and make their way round the course. It tips at one point and Mason jumps off to adjust it. He then continues on hands and knees with Declan following.

This was a long and quite complicated observation covering many aspects of the children's development. It might be easier to consider each child individually and divide your comments into different areas of development.

When you have completed your list of comments about the children, compare it with the suggestions given at the end of their observation. Try not to look too soon. You will notice that the list has been arranged into different areas of development. If you try to think in these terms you will probably find it easier to identify areas you wish to observe.

So now you have several reasons for observing these children. However, if you focus on one area of development you can look and record in more detail. Go back and look at the observation again. You can see that, although there is a lot happening, there are also lots of gaps. Unless you were looking for social interaction it would probably be better to concentrate on one child and look at one area of development – e.g. Communication and Language – Listening and attention and Understanding, Physical Development – Gross Motor, or Expressive Arts and Design – Creating with Materials and Being Imaginative and Expressive.

Suggestions for what you may have recorded about Mason and Declan

Mason:

Physical

- Good gross motor skills when handling large objects.
- Good eye–hand co-ordination when lining up objects.
- Able to balance and to crawl along narrow planks.

Intellectual

- Good concentration.
- Understands concept of balancing objects.
- Able to plan and carry out that plan, including testing the walkway.
- Language essentially correct in pronunciation and tense.

Social

- Able to work with another on a project but likes to be in control.
- Very determined when wanting to carry out his plan.

Dylan:

Physical

- Good control of gross motor skills when moving and placing large objects.
- Able to balance and crawl on narrow planks.

Intellectual

- Able to concentrate and take direction from another.
- Understands balance.

Social

- Able to work with a partner, following their direction.

Activity 2

When next in your nursery/school placement, select a single child or group and decide which area of development you want to observe.

Formulate your aim/focus, remembering to be precise.

Handy tip. If you are stuck for ideas, refer to *Development Matters* (DfE, 2020) or *Birth to 5 Matters* (Early Years Coalition, 2021). This should help you formulate your focus.

Remember, The aim/focus/purpose is just the formal way of setting out your plan to discover what children are able to do.

Your focus could be to see how children organize an activity. This could be written as:

Aim/focus: To observe a group of nursery children (aged 3 to 4 years) planning, in order to identify: how well the children work together, if all the children become involved and to see if any of the children become the leader.

Or your focus could be to see how good the children's physical abilities are:

Aim/focus: To observe the gross motor skills of a group of 5- to 6-year-olds engaged in physical play in the adventure playground, to identify how well they are able to balance; move between objects, control their movements when using the equipment.

Activity 3

Now that you have successfully formulated a variety of aims/focuses it is time to try out some of the observation techniques in your own workplace.

You could try out one of the aims you used for the last activity or construct new ones for the age group you work with. You will have noticed that the aims often refer to the age of the child, so it is important to record the child's date of birth. This is especially important in the younger age group, as there are a lot of changes taking place in a year. Your purpose for observing a child who is just 3 years old is unlikely to be the same as for a child who is 3 years 11 months old, as their development should be closer to that of a 4-year-old.

Then record the observations in order to use them for future activities.

You will now have a collection of observations covering the stages reached by the children in your age group. The next step is to consider what use you can make of them.

The first thing you need to consider is whether the aims have been met. This is discussed in the assessment by looking again at what you have observed and matching to what you hoped to find out. Of course you may not have met all your aims, but this does not matter. You can mention this in the assessment and suggest other follow-up observations you might need to do.

There follows another observation with an assessment. The format also includes details of the child and the setting, and the timing of the observation.

Observation

Name of child: Arabella

Age: 5 years and 2 months

Time commenced: 10.00 am   **Time completed:** 10.15 am

Setting: Reception class

Aim/focus/purpose: To discover if Arabella can recognize an amount without needing to count.

Record of observation

Arabella is sitting down with her class. Teacher asks the children to sit and listen carefully. She says, 'Can you show me two fists?' Arabella immediately raises both her hands, showing her fists. Teacher now asks, 'Can you show me four fingers?' Arabella looks around at the other children beside her. She slowly raises her right hand, showing four fingers. She starts to raise her left hand, but then quickly puts it back in her lap.

Teacher holds up a large dice. 'I want you to look at the number of spots I'm going to show you, and then show me the same number on your fingers.' She shows the side with three dots. Arabella looks at her left hand and lifts two fingers, appears to count them, and then raises a finger on the right hand and smiles.

Teacher tells all the children 'well done'.

Assessment of observation
Arabella enjoyed the activity and was able to confidently show her two fists. She showed some hesitation when showing four fingers and did appear to need to count her fingers for the dice numbers. She did recognize the number after observing the children around her, and appears to be on the verge of subitising.

You can see how the assessment summarizes what you have observed and relates the findings to the aim/focus.

Activity 4

Using the observations that you have completed, write assessments that summarize your findings and relate how they meet the aim/focus.

This activity almost completes what you should include in a written/narrative observation. You should now consider how observations can support your work practice, by underpinning your knowledge of child development in order to identify experiences that will lead them forward.

The value of observations is in their use, not just for a collection in a record-keeping file. We utilize the observation by evaluating it, comparing it with the expected developmental stage, and then making any recommendations. You should use recognized sources describing child development when you are comparing what you have observed against what is expected. See the following observation for an example.

Observation

Date: 8 October 2019

Time commenced: 10.15 am   **Time completed:** 10.35 am

Number of children: 3

Name and ages of children: 4 years 10 months, 5 years, 4 years 10 months, identified in observation as Child A, B and C.

Setting: Forest school - Wooded area. Children have the freedom to choose where they wish to explore and play. Class teacher and teaching assistant (TA) are monitoring and ensuring safety.

Aim/focus/purpose: To observe a group of children during outside play: to observe how the children interact and make use of their natural surroundings.

Record of observation

Children A, B and C are playing together. They have decided to make a hospital in a corner of the wooded area. They are deciding where would be the best place to start. They are careful to step over tree roots and avoid slopes.

Child A says, 'We can't have it there,' pointing to the tree, 'because there is no shelter.'

Child B says, 'We can put this over the top for shelter'; she pulls a large twig covered in leaves down over the base of the tree.

Child C says, 'We need a sign for the hospital' - she picks up two sticks and places them onto a leaf to make a cross. 'That's it, now everyone will be able to find the hospital.' Child C appears confident in her approach and moves on to talk about an ambulance.

Child B says, 'We need a stretcher - when I was in hospital I went on a stretcher.' She goes behind the tree to look for her materials. 'We need big leaves, something soft.'

Child B finds a leaf that is large and wide.

Child C finds a long narrow leaf.

Child B says, 'Mine is big it will be comfortable.'

Child C says, 'Mine is long so you can lie down on it.'

Child A has been listening and watching the other two girls. She says, 'We can make use of the big leaf as a cover on the bed.'

The other girls agree and return to the base of the tree to place their items.

The three children run over to the TA to tell her about the hospital. The TA moves over to the base of the tree and asks each child about what they have been doing. All the children are eager to relate their part in the process of making a hospital. They continue to look at their hospital and Child B suddenly says, 'When I went into hospital, I went into the Plaster Room - I hurt my arm and had to have plaster on it. My friends wrote their names on it.'

The other children listen carefully and decide to use a hole in the base of the tree for a plaster room.

Suddenly they hear the signal for finishing all activities. They walk back towards the Tepee and sit down on their logs to recall their morning's activities with the other children and adults in the group.

Assessment of observation

The three children worked well together, eager to add their own ideas but listened to each other's. They showed an awareness of safety when moving about. Each child appeared confident when they made a suggestion. Each time they needed to negotiate a situation they were patient and sorted out any differences quickly and amicably. Child B had experienced a hospital visit and was able to share it with the others. Child A thought about differences when the children were discussing the size and shape of the leaves and suggested a resolution so that both could be used. All the children appeared to enjoy their activity and share their contributions with the TA.

Reflection/analysis/forward planning

The children appear to be operating at the level expected for their age. This can be shown by comparing their actions and speech with the age ranges described in Development Matters in the EYFS.

Personal, social and emotional development

All the children were able to take part in the role-play, to initiate conversations and listen to others, and resolve any different ideas. They understood where they were able to go in the woods and when to stop play at the end of the session.

Communication and language – listening, attention and understanding

All the children were able to listen to each other and use ideas expressed by each other. They continued their play while listening, and talked through ideas to organize their role-play. Child B used her hospital experience to add ideas.

Physical development

The children collected and used the twigs and leaves in an appropriate way. They demonstrated an awareness of health and safety by avoiding tree roots and slopes when positioning their hospital. Although adults were nearby, they did not need to intervene to supervise.

Mathematics

The children understood the concept of big, small, long and wide when discussing their leaves.

Understanding the world

Child B used her experience of being to the hospital to extend the play.

The children explored their outdoor area when they collected the natural materials they needed.

Expressive arts and design

All the children worked collaboratively using the twigs and leaves to achieve their interpretation of a hospital.

The children were able to use their imagination; by using natural materials to create a hospital, they extended their play as new ideas emerged from each of the group.

Recommendations following reflection
The outdoor area provided an opportunity to work together in a team. This allowed the exploration of ideas through an activity with a theme, which enabled all the children to enjoy the spontaneous fun that occurred. Outdoor areas within the natural environment are an excellent setting for children to explore their own ideas without constraint. Where they are available, best use should always be made of outdoor areas. Indoor spaces used for role-play should also provide equipment that can be used in several ways, e.g. lengths of cloth.

Activity 5

You can now complete your observations and make final evaluations. Refer back to your aims, read through the observation, and check that you have summarized your findings in the assessment. Reflect on your findings and compare with expected development ranges for the age group. You can also research developmental theorists such as Chomsky for language and Piaget schemas.

When considering your evaluation, remember:

- Be specific in your comments.
- Try always to be objective and not make sweeping statements or assumptions.
- Identify where the child may be on their own developmental pathway.
- Make recommendations for further observation or activities in order to consider how to support a child moving forward in their development.

The exercises you have accomplished should have enabled you to complete your structured written/narrative observations – that is, observations which have been planned to discover the abilities of a child or children in a certain developmental area: observations which have pre-determined aims and objectives. Once you have been recording these for a while and discovered their value, you may want to use them to note language or behaviour that just happens around you. This would mean writing without specifically formulated objectives, although it is likely that what interested you was related to one prime area of development. This would be called an unplanned or unstructured written/narrative observation.

A less formal and more spontaneous way of observing is extensively used in settings. A spontaneous way of recording may capture an 'in the moment' or a 'wow' moment. A 'wow' moment usually includes photographs or video recording and is often written using Post-it notes. It can be a 'first' for a child or something particular to that child. These are usually brief moments. The 'moment' is then transferred to the learning journal or development folder for the child, and then shared later with his/her parents/carers.

The 'in the moment' form of observation is spontaneous but can be longer than a 'wow' moment. Teachers and Early Years practitioners note the scenario, the child's exact words, and where possible the level of engagement with the activity. The use of a camera, video recorder, school mobile phone or iPad can make the information easier to collect. The aim of collecting this information helps to inform future learning and support ongoing assessment. When completed, the observation and any photographs are transferred to the child's learning journal. This facilitates the sharing of information with parents and others in order to celebrate children's progress in the early years.

In fact, although it was unplanned, it should have some structure. The format should still include details of the child so that assessment, evaluations and recommendations can be made. See the following observation for an example.

Observation

Date: 16 October 2018

Names of children: Sophie plus four children

Ages: Sophie 4 years; three children (similar ages)

Time commenced: 2.00 pm   **Time completed:** 2.20 pm

Setting: Role-play area - in Reception class setting

Record of observation
Sophie is in the role-play area preparing to give a show to a group of children who have joined her. They are sitting on the carpet ready to be the audience. Sophie is in a long skirt and wears a magician's hat. She collects together all her props.

She does not ask for any adult help - she is certain what she needs. When she is ready, she stands confidently in front of her audience. She has a small rabbit puppet on her right hand, and she holds it up towards her face, next to her ear. She is motionless, listening to her puppet. After a few quiet moments, she says in a higher pitched voice, 'Oh, do you want to talk to the audience?' She makes the puppet nod its hand and head and listens again for her next instruction. 'Oh, you want to go in the hat and disappear. Right ladies and gentleman the rabbit will go in my hat and disappear.'

She puts the rabbit into the hat, and hides the rabbit inside a pocket in the hat then shows the audience the empty hat. 'Look the rabbit has gone.'

She shakes the hat and then makes the rabbit appear again. She has an amused look on her face and bows to the audience. They all clap and she walks away with a large smile on her face.

Sophie walks back to her stage and looks at the audience. She stands for a minute holding the puppet up to her face. The children who were watching stay in their position on the floor waiting to see what happens. Sophie walks to the children, holds the puppet near to them and says, 'You want to talk to the children. What do you want to say?' She looks at the children. 'He wants to know if you want him to disappear again - do you?'

The children say, 'Yes,' and she proceeds to put the puppet back into the hat and repeats the performance. The children clap again and Sophie walks off.

Assessment of observation
This observation gave a completely different insight into Sophie's personality. She is usually a quiet, shy girl in the setting and waits before offering to join in activities.

When Sophie used the props, she had an awareness of her own role as magician, the role of the puppet, and an awareness of how they both needed to interact and entertain the audience.

Sophie was also aware of changing her tone of voice; she is able to differentiate between each character and the audience while maintaining her own character. It appears that she felt more confident by stepping into the role of magician, wearing props and changing her tone of voice.

Reflection/analysis

During her role-play, Sophie demonstrated that her development is well within expected ranges for her age. Comparing with the development statements of the EYFS can show this.

Personal, social and emotional development

Sophie is normally quiet, but she was able to adapt her behaviour in order to confidently take on the role of the magician.

Communication and language

Sophie was able to pretend to listen to the puppet, maintain her role as the magician, and speak for the puppet.

Sophie used language in the role-play to explain to her audience what she was doing. She was also able to project language onto the puppet; listening to what he was meant to say and then telling the children.

Expressive arts and design

Sophie was fully engaged in the role-play, using language she may have heard on the television. She chose her props to support what she wanted to say and do in the role of magician.

Recommendations following reflection

This observation shows that the environmental setting can provide the opportunity for children to succeed and show a level of confidence far exceeding their normal persona in a different environment. Children may be capable and confident but need a variety of settings to be able to feel secure and display their skills.

Observations have provided evidence that Sophie now needs encouragement to participate in a variety of role-play situations to build on her confidence and self-esteem. She will be able to join in with other children and enjoy their company, develop her skills and work towards the Early Learning Goal.

The second observation of an 'in the moment' event is of Oliver after he sees a friend with a plastic fake ketchup sachet and tomato stain.

Observation

Date: 16 October 2020

Names and ages of children: Oliver - 4 years and 10 months, child A - 5 years and 2 months, child B - 4 years and 3 months.

Setting: Reception class

Record of observation
Oliver says, 'It's a joke - can I do it?' Child A gives the fake packet and stain to Oliver who lays the joke stain on the floor. 'Oh, I have spilt sauce on the floor.' Both children look down and giggle. Child A is aware of the joke and indulges Oliver by giving attention and smiling. Oliver takes the fake sauce over to where another younger child (B) is playing with loose play equipment. He places the stain on the floor and exclaims, 'Oh no - I dropped the sauce.' This time it is said in a serious voice. Child B doesn't speak and looks worried. They both look round to see if anyone is watching. Oliver begins to giggle, 'Fooled you, it's a joke.' They both laugh and child B picks up the 'plastic sauce'. They study it together, 'It's a joke' says child B.

Assessment of observation
Oliver was aware of the joke from his own experiences of thinking, guessing and knowing. He was able to share the experience with a younger child who did not fully understand the concept of

a 'joke', unlike the older child who was able to fully appreciate the humour of the 'wow moment' they shared.

Oliver enjoys playing tricks and jokes, and likes an audience to help with the enjoyment of the humour. Richard Woolfson, a child psychologist, writes that 'humour is an important part of nursery/school life, creating a relaxed, pleasant atmosphere, helping children to bond with each other' (Nursery World, February 2000).

Reflection/analysis/forward planning
In the observations of Sophie and Oliver, the aim was to capture the interest of children in the present moment, to encourage the children's natural instinct to learn explore and question, then extend their learning with extension activities in an enabling environment. Careful observations are a key to utilizing the approach to build on the children's needs, recognized as a 'teachable moment. In the moment planning is then carried out to plan a topic, spontaneously based on what a child is interested in. The setting where the observations were undertaken used them to plan how to set up an outside area as a travelling theatre, including a stage and audience seating. A variety of props, including cameras and clothing, were made available for the children to express their artistic talents in any way they wished.

Enabling and supporting laughter during childhood gives children an important skill for life. Children will benefit from humour and laughter as they experience awe and wonder activities. They will also come to understand the realization that beliefs do not necessarily match reality and that different people hold a variety of beliefs.

In Development Matters children aged 3 to 4 years old are able to express a point of view, and debate and disagree with a friend using words and actions. They are able to start a conversation with a friend and continue it for many turn takings in order to organize their play. Oliver understands the language used: 'It's a joke, fooled you.' He acknowledged the children's different reactions and involved them both in the fun of the joke.

Practitioners should provide opportunities to listen, and to talk about a variety of experiences in order to build a familiarity and understanding of humour.

Enabling environments for promoting self-esteem

Adults can:

- Make materials accessible so that children are able to imagine and develop their projects and ideas while they are still fresh in their minds and important to them.

- Provide for, initiate and join in imaginative play and role-play, encouraging children to talk about what is happening and to act out the scenarios in character.

- Plan regular short periods when individuals listen to others, such as singing a short song, sharing an experience or describing something they have seen or done.

In practice, in your work place, these assessments, analysis and recommendations may be verbal, but they should become a valuable tool for planning for individual need.

You have therefore made use of your observation even though you had no set objectives at the outset. It cannot be stressed too often that observations are tools to be used to assist your learning and provide a basis for planning children's progression. They are essential for completing the EYFS profile and for using as a basis for discussion with parents.

Helen Sutherland and Angie Maxey (2014) state: 'It is important for Early Years Teachers to lead practitioners in their understanding of the observation process, so that they recognize the value and importance of observations in contributing to the assessment process.'

A Guide to Presenting and Experimenting with Observational Techniques

3

-
-

Now that you have had the opportunity to practise the art of observing and interpreting the information gained from the written/narrative format, it is time to look at the variety of other methods in more detail.

As a student working towards a qualification in Early Years Education, you are fortunate to have the opportunity to try a wide range of methods, and to gain a realistic awareness of their strengths and weaknesses.

Observation formats

Described below are four formats that can be used: diagrammatic, sampling, written and checklists. From these you should be able to see the knowledge that can be gained by observing children in a structured way. Whichever method chosen to carry out your observation, however, will require the same preliminary information (date, time, name, age). This will allow an informed assessment and reflection to be made.

When studying how children progress in their development, one reason to carry out an observation might be to see if the children described are following the expected path. This may be planned or could be a spontaneous 'in the moment' decision when you noticed the way a child is responding to a challenge. You will also be studying theorists, and observing children can allow you to discuss their ideas in an informed way.

Once the observation is completed, you would normally make an assessment and reflect, analyse and forward plan. This is often based around the EYFS developmental charts and reflections from your own work practice.

Remember that your assessment should be based on knowledge of child development and should never be judgmental. You also need to remember that children of a similar age may have had different experiences, resulting in different strengths and weaknesses. Your observation may give you the opportunity to provide suitable activities to build on these.

Your reflection should be for the benefit of the child – you are looking at what they can do, and then how to build on that. For instance, if you are observing behaviour that is giving cause for concern, then you should be looking for recommendations that will assist the child to have a more positive experience.

If you feel that you have not achieved what you set out to discover by your observation, then you may need to repeat it or try another method.

Figures 3.1 to 3.4 set out some of the formats for recording observations that are commonly used, followed by suggestions for when you might use the information given in Chapter 1.

Diagrammatic

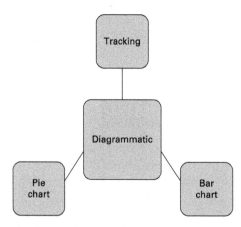

Figure 3.1 Observation format: diagrammatic.

Tracking: Observing and recording a child or children's movements around a limited area for a period of time, e.g. at nursery, the in classroom, in the playground.

Bar chart: A pictorial method of recording an observation of a whole group's ability to undertake a specific task, or a way of showing blocks of time spent on an activity.

Pie chart: An alternative pictorial method of recording a time-sampling observation or bar chart.

Sampling

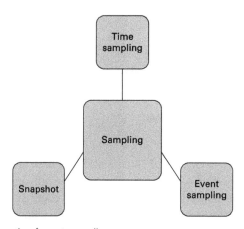

Figure 3.2 Observation format: sampling.

Time sampling: Observing and recording what a child is doing every minute for a short time, e.g. ten minutes, or at intervals during a set period of time, e.g. every fifteen minutes over a morning.

Event sampling: Observing and recording certain events as they occur, e.g. aggressive behaviour or temper tantrums.

Snapshot: Observing and recording events at a particular moment. They are useful for comparing use of equipment at different times of the day or monitoring play areas in order to make the best use of equipment. This type of observation is commonly recorded on sticky note or iPad, and is used to update a child's records or provide evidence for online planning.

Written

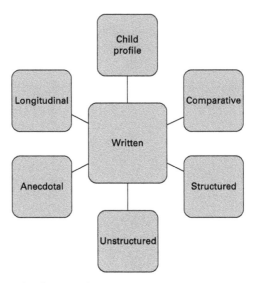

Figure 3.3 Observation format: written.

Child profile: Observing a child over a period of time to evaluate their overall developmental progress. This will normally include some details of the child's background and always needs parental permission. This may contribute to the child's summative assessment.

Longitudinal: This is an extended child profile, usually for six to twelve months and is normally used when observing babies during their first year of life when many changes are occurring.

Comparative: There are two main types of comparative observation: observing two children to compare the way they use an object, or observing one child over a period of time to evaluate progress.

Structured: Observing and recording for a purpose with pre-planned objectives, e.g. to discover a child's physical abilities when first entering the setting.

Unstructured: Observing children without a pre-determined purpose.

Checklists

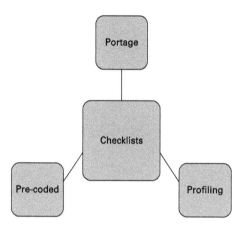

Figure 3.4 Observation format: checklists.

Pre-coded: Observing and recording specific aspects of development using a pre-coded checklist of developmental milestones. This could be an individual observation, but often forms part of an overall and ongoing profile of the child.

Profiling: The profiling record of children can consist of checklists that are supported by short written observations. This allows a practitioner to comment on how and when a child achieves and makes progress.

Portage: Checklists are also commonly used when working with children with additional needs, in order to monitor their progress. Portage is a system that breaks down developmental milestones into smaller steps. These are used when developing a plan for the practitioner and parent to work with the child. Checklists are then used to monitor how successfully the targets are being met. This enables the practitioner and parent to set new targets or redefine the task.

Other recording methods

You might also consider using different media to help you record your observation. However, as the child may be clearly identified, this should always be discussed with your supervisor and the child's parents in the interest of confidentiality.

Figure 3.5 shows some of the different recording media you might use.

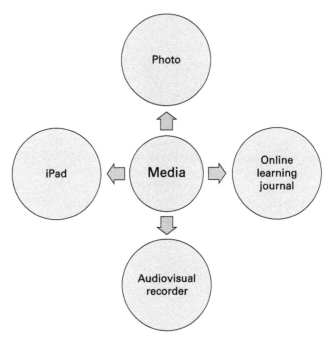

Figure 3.5 Recording using other media.

Commercial products for building a record of a child's experiences and development using an online learning journal are widely available. Using video, diaries and photos enables the teacher, early years practitioner and parent to work together to 'weave' a story of how the child is progressing. Increasingly, settings are moving towards online packages to support assessment. Observations are recorded on tablets and uploaded immediately to online platforms. Typical features include linking observations to EYFS areas of learning and development, the ability to collect data at the individual's level, and the facility to share data with parents on a secure line platform. These tools make analysis of data easier and quicker, as they link directly to different areas of the curriculum. Staff observations of children are used to assess how individual children are progressing. Data collected can prompt reviews of whether activities are meeting the needs of individual children, and whether activities and planning across the setting need improving. One of the advantages of the record sharing is that parents can be closely involved, as they are a valuable resource when assessing a child's development. They know their children intimately and have background information that will have a definite impact on how the child works through a variety of experiences and environments. The *Teach Early Years* magazine states that:

efficient reporting and in-depth data analysis can be uploaded by parents in real time, thereby sharing precious moments. The interactive online learning journal can record and track individual children's wellbeing, learning journey, milestones, experiences, and development. This interactive method can help manage how staff write and record, it feeds into professional development, helping staff to improve observations and planning to support the children's development.

Students will discuss in class the use of online programmes and will be encouraged to learn from their placement how the technology works, but normally they may not be directly using this kind of technology until they are in employment.

Observational techniques in practice

Diagrammatic: tracking

As stated in Chapter 1, the usual reason for undertaking a tracking observation is to record the amount of time a child spends on an activity or the number of activities they choose. The following example illustrates its use to track a child to discover motor skills on a choice of activities. Before commencing you would need to sketch a plan or take a photograph of the area you are going to observe the child in. You will need to consider how you are going to record the movement, e.g. do you need to devise a code? You will also need to consider what you want to find out, and how the child is meeting this. In the example in Chapter 1 the aims and purpose were connected to the time the child spent on the activity, so it was important to note the times on the diagram. In the following example you will see that the principal aim/purpose is to discover which apparatus is chosen, so there is no need to note time spent using it. However, in this case, there is a second reason for the observation: to identify the skills used on the apparatus. There is not usually space on the diagram to write this, especially if you identify difficulties. You will therefore need to record this separately.

Observation

Date: 11 December 2019

Time commenced: 10.50 am   **Time completed:** 11.05 am

Number of adults: 2   **Number of children:** Whole class

Name of child: Edward

DOB: 11 October 2014   **Age:** 5 years and 2 months

Setting: School hall set out for PE lesson to be used by whole class

Aim/focus/purpose: To observe a 5-year-old in a formally arranged setting of the gym in school hall to 1) track choice of activities and 2) identify and record Edward's gross motor skills using apparatus.

Record of observation
The easiest way to show the arrangement of the apparatus in the gym would be to take a photograph. You can then comment on which apparatus were chosen by Edward, and how successful he was. In this instance Edward chooses to use the ropes and climbing frame, but avoids the hoops and horse.

Ropes: Some difficulty climbing onto the end of the rope and not able to swing successfully but spends several minutes trying.

Climbing frame: Most time spent here. Climbs quite well initially, moving alternate arms and legs, but rather hesitant near to top of the frame. Descending rather difficult. Edward feels carefully for each rung before moving.

Assessment of observation
From the tracking observation, it is obvious that Edward prefers to work on the large apparatus - either the climbing frame or ropes, and avoids the hoops, horse and mat. Edward found difficulty in climbing onto the knot of the rope and then swinging. On the climbing frame he moved alternate arms and legs, reaching up above his head with arms extended, and carefully watching where he was going. He appeared more hesitant and apprehensive when near the top of the frame. The higher he climbed, the less fluent his movements were, and he stopped several times

to watch other children. He climbed down haltingly, feeling for each rung before making a move.

Reflection/analysis
According to Development Matters guidance (DfE, 2020) in the EYFS, children aged 4 to 5 years: 'Confidently and safely use a range of large and small apparatus indoors and outside, alone and in a group.'

Although Edward is keen to participate in these activities and likes to use the large apparatus, he has not yet gained confidence and is not able to move fluently, as most children of this age would be able to do. The majority of the class enjoyed the vigorous physical play and used their bodies confidently and actively. Edward appeared hesitant and enjoyed activities where he had some success, returning to these, unlike many 5-year-olds who are keen to master new skills and practise until they perfect them.

Forward planning
Edward needs more activities that will allow him to practise skills and gain confidence. He needs praise and encouragement to try new apparatus.
Another suggestion could be building confidence using different activities such as role-play, which also involves outdoor opportunities for physical development.

Note: This record shows very clearly the value of observing children as individuals. In the general rush of the class activity it is easy to miss the fact that one child is having some difficulty. Experienced workers will usually spot that a child needs some extra encouragement, but it is always useful to have recorded proof.

Diagrammatic: bar chart

In Chapter 1 we looked at the bar chart as a method of recording a class's ability to complete a task. In the following example the bar chart is used to give a pictorial representation of the time spent on different activities during a typical day at a nursery for a 7-month-old baby.

The times are recorded throughout the day and then transferred to the bar chart.

Observation

Date: 27 February 2020

Time commenced: 8.00 am   **Time completed:** 5.00 pm

Number of adults: 3

Number of children: 1 (6 other babies in nursery)

Name of child: Marc   **Age:** 7 months

Setting: Baby room and outdoor area of day nursery.

Aim/focus/purpose: To observe the care plan of a 7-month-old baby in a nursery setting throughout the day, by recording in minutes the time spent on social care and play on a typical day.

8.00-8.10 am: arrives at nursery for handover (exchange of information with parent)

8.10-8.30 am: freeplay inside with soft toys

8.30-8.45 am: painting activity

8.45-8.50 am: hand washing

8.50-9.15 am: freeplay outside

9.15-9.30 am: stories and songs

9.30-9.45 am: nappy changing and hand washing

9.45-10.30 am: snack and bottle of formula

10.30-12.00 pm: sleep

12.00-12.30 pm: freeplay

12.30-12.45 pm: nappy change and hand washing

12.45 pm-1.15 pm: lunch

1.15-2.15 pm: outing to the park

2.15-2.30 pm: nappy change and hand washing

2.30-3.30 pm: sleep

3.30-4.00 pm: waterplay

4.00-4.30 pm: snack and formula feed

4.30-5.00 pm: freeplay

5.00 pm: collected by parent and information exchanged

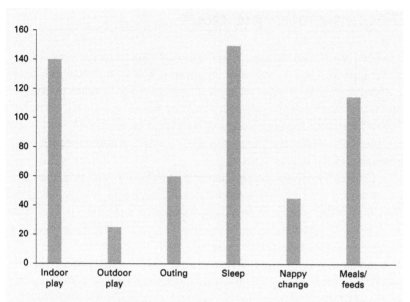

Figure 3.6 Bar chart showing time spent in minutes on each activity throughout the day.

Reflection/analysis/forward planning

The daycare programme followed at this nursery is very similar to one recommended by Patricia Geraghty (1988), who states in the section covering planning a child's day: 'The core of the programme for the young child in daycare is play, balanced by regular times allotted for routine purposes such as washing, lunch, snacks and a rest period.'

A baby of 7 months should follow the wishes of parents: in this case, two bottle feeds, finger feeding and sleep twice a day. Information was exchanged at the start and end of the day, which helps to build strong partnerships between practitioners and parents. This provides opportunities for a positive start when providing and planning for a variety of learning experiences.

There was plenty of opportunity for different types of play and social interaction, with a good staff ratio.

In order to evaluate the quality of the child's daily routine, some detailed written/narrative observations could be undertaken to provide evidence for planning for progression.

Diagrammatic: pie chart

Pie charts are a pictorial way of showing a period of time, or a number of children, divided into a percentage of a whole. This is presented as a circle (360 degrees). Data showing amounts of time, numbers of subjects, types of objects etc. can usually be demonstrated using a bar chart or a pie chart. The previous bar chart, showing amount of time spent on different activities in a day, could also be divided into percentages of time in a nine-hour period and presented as a pie chart.

In Chapter 1 we showed a pie chart as a way of illustrating percentages of a class who could carry out a procedure. In this example we are using the chart to show the amount of time a child spends on different activities. This can cover any length of time, but in practice is usually shorter when observing younger children, as their attention span is likely to be shorter.

A certain amount of information about the child's concentration could be gathered by simply noting the time spent on each activity and converting into the pie chart, but this would not allow much opportunity for reflection. By adding written comments, you will have more evidence on which to base comments and reflection in order to help the child progress. This will be much more useful when completing their records and provide the basis for planning within the nursery or reception class.

Observation

Date: 12 February 2020

Time commenced: 10.45 am   Time completed: 10.55 am

Number of adults: 1   Number of children: 3

Name of child: Joseph   Age: 3 years 6 months

Setting: Quiet area of the nursery, set out with various activities.

Aim/focus/purpose: To observe a 3-year and 6 month old during a free choice session to record his concentration span at different activities.

Record of observation
Joseph waits as the other children decide where they would like to work before moving.

Activity a (2 minutes): Joseph stands looking round and then moves to home corner. He takes a dish out of the cupboard and then searches through the food basket. He decides on the pizza, which he puts onto the dish and into the oven. After a moment he says, 'It's hot now.' He goes over to the drawer and takes out the oven glove, which he uses to remove the pizza from the oven. He puts it onto the table, takes off the glove and walks away.

Activity b (2 minutes): Joseph walks round the room and finally stops at the Lego. He puts both hands into the box and moves the bricks around while watching Daniel, who is building a tower. He moves over to the doll's house and watches as Matthew replaces the bedroom furniture.

Activity c (1 minute): Joseph moves back to the Lego and fixes two pieces together then walks round looking at what others are doing, before returning to the doll's house.

Activity d (1 minute): Joseph picks up a ladder and carefully places it between the two floors of the house. He moves around on his knees then stands up and moves away. He wanders around and EYP asks if he would like to do a puzzle. He nods and follows her back to the table.

Activity e (3 minutes): Joseph sits down at the table with the EYP. He tips the pieces out of the puzzle board and starts to look for the right spaces to put them back. He does not require help, but looks to the EYP for encouragement at intervals. He completes the puzzle and smiles.

Activity f (1 minute): Joseph goes over to the train set and crouches down. He watches as Matthew pushes the train along the track, then walks back to the home corner.

Reflection/analysis

When the result of the observation is shown as a pie chart covering the ten-minute period, it demonstrates clearly that Joseph did not stay with an activity for long.

Time spent

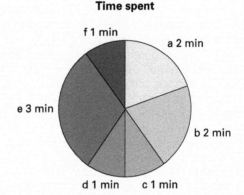

Figure 3.7 Pie chart showing time spent on activities.

When given a free choice of activities, Joseph took some time choosing. When he had chosen an activity, it did not hold his concentration for long. With the attention of an adult, he was able to concentrate for longer and complete a task.

Joseph has only been attending the nursery for half a term and still appears overwhelmed by the choices available. After he received guidance, he appeared reassured and sat and concentrated longer. Having only been in nursery for a short time, he is still only beginning to explore and would rather stand and watch what the other children are doing.

He says very little and appears not to have reached the stage where he can 'Play with one or more other children, extending and elaborating play ideas', nor does he yet 'become more outgoing with unfamiliar people, in the safe context of their setting' (Development Matters 'Personal, social and emotional development: Making relationships, three to four years').

Forward planning
Joseph will benefit from some guidance when given choices, or to be offered less choice in order to extend his concentration span. He also needs to be encouraged to join in small group activities such as sand and water play, which have several opportunities for interaction.

Sampling: time sampling – target child

As described in Chapter 1, time sampling is used to record a series of short observations over a varied period of time. It is almost always planned to answer a question about an individual child, or a group if considering language or social interaction.

The main advantage of the method is that long periods of time can be covered. It also allows for flexibility, e.g. you could choose to observe the same hour at the beginning of the week and the end to see if children are acting differently. The main disadvantage is that the actions/behaviours you wish to observe may not be taking place when you have chosen to observe. Also, it is easy to become distracted by other needs when you are using intervals of fifteen or thirty minutes.

The following example covers a period of ten minutes each day during freeplay to observe how one child chooses activities and socializes over the period of a week.

Observation

Date: 2-6 March 2020

Time commenced: 9.35 am   **Time completed:** 9.45 am

Number of adults: 3   **Number of children:** 7-10

Name of child: Kaitlin   **Age:** 3 years 2 months

Setting: Outdoors area of a day nursery during a period of free play. Children have a selection of equipment and apparatus.

Aim/focus/purpose: To observe Kaitlin, who attends nursery five mornings a week, over a period of ten minutes each day, during outdoors free play in order to:

- monitor choices made;
- observe skills demonstrated.

Record of observation

9.30 am, 2-6 March: Each morning Kaitlin's room group is asked to put on their coats ready to go outside. This is an area divided into: grass section where there are materials for large construction e.g. tyres, planks of wood, crates, drums; a tarmacked area with bikes, scooters, cars, prams, and a large sandpit with buckets, spades, sieves and toys. There is also a garden area where the children can dig, ready for spring planting.

9.35-9.45 am, 2 March: Kaitlin has chosen to ride on a tricycle. She puts her feet on the pedals but fails to make them turn. She places her feet on the ground and uses them to push herself forward. By moving back and forward she is able to travel in a straight line but finds steering difficult. After a couple of minutes she gets off and walks away.

9.35-09.45 am, 3 March: Kaitlin is sitting on the tricycle. She has her feet on the pedals and with great effort manages to push one down and move slightly forward. She now appears stuck and resumes, using her feet to push along.

9.35-9.45 am, 4 March: Today it is pouring with rain so the children are not able to go out.

9.35-09.45, 5 March: Kaitlin is waiting for a child to vacate a tricycle. She watches as he uses the pedals to move and handlebars to steer. When he gets off, she climbs on and puts her feet on the pedals. She pushes her right foot down and moves a little then gets stuck. The EYP notices her problem and offers help by pushing the bike while Kaitlin uses the pedals. When she is well underway, the EYP stops pushing and Kaitlin manages to keep going for several feet. She appears pleased and smiles. She tries again and, using a lot of effort, she manages to turn the pedals unassisted.

Assessment of observation
During the periods of observation, Kaitlin chose to play on the tarmac area. She enjoyed the tricycle and made great strides, achieving the ability to use the pedals to propel herself by the end of the week. There was not much language heard, but any words and sounds were used in the correct context.

Reflection/analysis/forward planning
According to Development Matters for the EYFS, a 3-year-old will 'Continue to develop their

movement, balancing, riding (scooters, trikes and bikes) and ball skills". Kaitlin progressed from using her feet to move the tricycle to being able to use the pedals. She should be praised for her efforts and encouraged to steer round corners.

Personal, Social and Emotional development can 'Select and use activities and resources, with help when needed. This helps them to achieve a goal they have chosen, or one which is suggested to them.' Kaitlin was able to choose where she wanted to play and with what resources. She was willing to wait for the tricycle. She could be encouraged to take part in group activities such as parachute.

Communication and Language - Understanding and Speaking. 'Use a wider range of vocabulary', 'understand a question or instruction that has two parts, such as: "Get your coat and wait at the door".'

Kaitlin used very little language, but she did listen to instructions and questions.

The resources chosen by Kaitlin did not require much interaction with other children or adults. If staff have not heard language in other situations this would suggest that a longer observation should be undertaken. Her understanding and ability to follow directions do not seem in doubt. It would be useful to ask parents if she is chattier at home.

Sampling: event sampling

Event sampling is usually linked to observations of children who have a tendency to behave in anti-social ways, such as temper tantrums beyond what is normal and bullying. The purpose is to record any incident; if possible what preceded it, and what followed. Child psychologists often use this technique, known as ABC, short for Antecedent, Behaviour and Consequence.

Observation

Date: 17 January 2020   **Time:** Throughout the day

Number of adults: 2   **Number of children:** 26

Name of child: Ben   **Age:** 4 years 5 months

Setting: Reception class

Aim/focus/purpose: To observe Ben's behaviour throughout the day in order to:

- record any incidents of unsociable behaviour;
- identify any triggers for the behaviour;
- record what follows the incident.

Record of observation

Time	Behaviour	Antecedent	Who was present	Consequence	Comment
11.20 am	Ben snatches a pencil from James, and James takes it back	Ben and James in the art area using colouring pencils to draw a picture of their choosing	Two other children also present at the table and EYP close by	Ben calls James a name and hits him on the arm. James shouts out and EYP intervenes. She asks Ben to say sorry for hitting	Ben needs to learn that it is not acceptable to just take what he wants. He needs to control his anger and ask adult for help
11.25 am	Previous incident repeated	Colouring quietly again after previous incident addressed	Ben and James alone at the table. EYP in the book corner	James calls the EYP and tells her what has happened. Ben moved to other side of table and given own set of pencils	Ben reminded again to ask before taking

Time	Behaviour	Antecedent	Who was present	Consequence	Comment
1.20 pm	Elliot pushes Ben from behind, causing him to fall	Children getting changed for a music and movement activity	All the children are changing into PE kit and the EYP assisting where necessary	Ben jumps up and pulls Elliot's jumper. Elliot shouts and EYP intervenes to find out what has occurred	In this instance Ben was not the instigator of the incident but needs to ask an adult for help
1.50 pm	Ben screams because he thinks someone has his socks. He runs round picking up socks and throwing them	Children changing back after the activity	All the children and teacher and EYP present	Several children back away, looking scared. NN intervenes, finds socks and asks Ben to sit at one side to dress	Ben needs help to find an acceptable way to express himself

Assessment of observation

Ben reacted very quickly when other children upset him. He showed little consideration for others' needs and took what he wanted without asking or negotiating. Ben used very little language throughout the day, tending to demonstrate his feelings with actions. However, although the reaction was not acceptable, Ben was not always the instigator of the incident.

Reflection/analysis/forward planning

According to EYFS Development Matters - 'Managing Self and Building Relationships', 3- and 4-year-olds 'Help to find solutions to conflicts and rivalries' and 'Talk with others to solve conflicts'. By the time they are entering reception they should be able to: 'Identify and moderate their own feelings socially and emotionally'.

According to Stanford Children's Health, 'Your Child's Social and Emotional Development', by the end of the third year your child should be able to play simple games, take turns and recognize concepts such as 'yours' and 'mine'.

By the end of the fourth year your child should have enough self-control to negotiate through conflicts.

Ben did not demonstrate an ability to use self-regulatory skills towards his peers or understand sharing, and the concept of 'yours' and 'mine'. Self-regulatory skills can be defined as the ability of children to manage their own behaviour and aspects of their learning, in order to improve levels of self-control and reduce impulsivity. Ben showed little understanding of negotiating and compromise to resolve a conflict. He is not quite 4, but his inability to use words rather than physical aggression is not usual at this age. However, the other children do seem to have learned this and can provoke Ben to retaliate.

Ben demonstrated little understanding of realizing that actions cause distress to others. He finds it difficult to share without the support of an adult.

Ben's behaviour definitely falls outside of the normal limits of the developmental stages described in *Development Matters* and other publications.

When considering recommendations, it is very important that all adults understand the importance of consistency in any behaviour modification programme. The nursery SENCO will be able to help by working with staff to establish a programme for everyone to follow. This will mean that Ben's behaviour will be treated consistently while in the nursery. The programme should also be discussed fully with parents, who may have their own strategies for coping if Ben is also demonstrating the behaviour at home. As stated in section 7 of the introduction to *Development Matters* (DfE, 2020), the help that parents give their children at home has a very significant impact on their learning.

The programme may include:

- Rewarding Ben when his behaviour is acceptable: 'Catch them being good'.
- Encouraging Ben to express his feelings in acceptable ways using clay, water, role-play etc.
- Listening to both children's explanations after an incident.

Present practice in schools and nurseries aims to devise ways to encourage self-regulation and build resilience. Resilient children will develop protective skills but need supportive environments that help them cope with difficult situations.

Written

The structured and unstructured forms of written narrative were described fully in Chapter 2. We will now consider some of the other forms listed.

Comparative

The comparative observation can compare two children of the same age at the same time. This might cover their ability to complete a task or assess their physical skills. One needs to be careful that the comparison is linked to recognized developmental norms, rather than comparing children against each other. You need to remember that observations are for the benefit of each individual child. It would perhaps be more useful to compare one child over a period of time. This could be another way to record the observation of the child in the earlier time sampling example, or the tracking observation in the school hall. It would remove the time constraint and could cover longer than a week if necessary. In this instance the comparison observation follows Edward who experienced some difficulties in the gym (see previous tracking Observation, pages 54–5).

The comparative observation will demonstrate if the forward planning has helped him to succeed.

Observation

Time commenced: 10.50   **Time completed:** 11.05 am

Number of adults: 2   **Number of children:** 26

Name of child: Edward

DOB: 11 October 2014   **Age:** 5 years 5 months

Setting: School hall set out for PE lesson to be used by whole class. Climbing frame and ropes are fixed. Ramp, horse and mat are free standing. Children may also choose hoops and balls.

Aim/purpose/focus: To observe Edward's choice of equipment and identify gross motor skills following three months in school to compare his progress.

Record of observation

Edward runs over to the ropes and takes hold of one. He confidently steps up onto the knotted end and manages to reach up and then pull up his legs. He does this twice before sliding down. He moves over to the ramp and manages to put his right leg over the horse and pull himself up to sit on it. Another child runs up the ramp and Edward slides off onto the mat.

Edward walks over to the climbing frame. Using alternate feet and arms he confidently climbs to the top and looks down to see who is following. He descends, feeling for the rungs as he goes.

Back on the floor a child throws a ball to him, which he catches with both hands.

Assessment of observation

Edward is able to use the large equipment with confidence. He is learning to climb the rope using arms and legs and was able to sit on the horse. He managed to climb to the top of the climbing frame without hesitation using alternate arms and legs. He descended by safely feeling for the rungs, without the need to look down. On the ground he was able to catch a ball thrown by another child.

Reflection/analysis
Edward has demonstrated that he has moved forward in his confidence and gross motor ability since he was last observed, three months ago. The practice he has received has enabled him to improve his skills, and now he is following the guidance that the 4- to 5-year-old is 'confidently and safely able to use a range of large and small apparatus' indoors and outside, alone and in a group' (Development Matters guidance, 2020).

Forward planning
Following Edward's progress, continue to offer opportunities to help him refine his skills. As the weather improves, make the best use of outdoor spaces for games and freeplay.

Progress charts and child profiles

Child profiles can be undertaken in any format. Children born in England and Wales will automatically have a record book, generated at birth, for health professionals to record weight, immunizations, developmental checks, etc.

The personal health record (PCHR) also often referred to as 'The Red Book' will move with the family in order that continuity is maintained. Most parents also keep a record of first smile, steps and words.

Within the nursery and reception class, formal assessments of progress are made in the child's second year, and in the summer term before the commencement of Key Stage 1. This profile is an assessment of the three characteristics of learning and seventeen Early Learning Goals. Evidence can come from staff, parents and the child themselves. There is no designated format for the profile, but it should be able to demonstrate everything that the child has achieved. In the past this might all have been kept in the child's personal file, consisting of observations, child's work, photos, etc. It is much more likely now that establishments will have bought into commercial record keeping products that allow staff and parents to share their knowledge digitally. Photos, observations, children's work can all be stored within the system ready to be recalled when necessary. This allows for instant updates to be made, and for all staff to be aware if children's programmes are changed.

Detailed profiles for an ongoing child study are normally only undertaken when there is a concern in an area of development. This may be in one area, such as speech, or cover a general developmental delay. Case studies will always contain details of the child and background information such as any birth trauma experienced.

For study purposes, students may undertake a longitudinal observation of development over a period of a year. This will often be in the first year of a child's life as much is happening in the areas of physical and social changes. There has been some interesting research undertaken by Flensborg-Madsen and Mortensen (2017) indicating that both pre- and post-natal factors are predictors of age of attaining milestones in infancy: 'Several individual factors, especially gestational age, birth weight, breastfeeding, having lived in a long-term institution, and weight and head increase in the first year, were significantly associated with milestone attainment in the first year of life.'

Methods of recording for a longitudinal observation, and the interval between recordings will depend on the original reason for undertaking the study.

Sociologists studying groups of children may carry out the observations by questionnaire or interview, and these may continue at yearly intervals for many years. Children being monitored for a specific reason, such as a speech delay or defect, may require monthly monitoring to assess progress.

For the purpose of undertaking a longitudinal observation as part of your studies, it would probably be most practical to work with the parent, who can tell you about changes they have observed. You would only need to make your own observation at intervals. Also, if willing, they could take photographs that would provide evidence of using other media to record.

The following example is a longitudinal study undertaken over a period of nine months. The reason for monitoring progress was that he was born at thirty-two weeks' gestation.

Initial interview with mother Brigit

Mark was born at St. George's maternity hospital on 6 August 2019. He was due to be born on 1 October, so his actual gestational age was thirty-two weeks at delivery.

Until the beginning of August, the pregnancy was progressing normally but on the 1st Brigit went into premature labour.

She was admitted to hospital and on 6 August Mark was born. He breathed immediately, but as his weight was only 1.9 kg he was moved to the neonatal unit in an incubator.

After an initial weight loss, Mark started to gain weight from day seven. His sucking reflex was poor, so he was still being tube fed and nursed in oxygen.

On day fourteen Mark stopped breathing. He was quickly resuscitated but it was discovered that his lungs had collapsed. The cause was unknown but Mark needed to be put on a ventilator. He was given antibiotics as a precaution.

Mark breathed for himself after four days, but he had two more episodes requiring ventilation, and concerns were expressed about any long-term effects of the pressure on his lungs.

On 17 September, when Mark was six weeks old, he was transferred to a cot. He gained weight and was discharged home on 26 September.

With Brigit's consent, a series of observations were arranged for key stages in first year development to see if there were any lasting effects from the traumatic birth and early breathing problems.

First observation

Date: 1 October 2019

Time commenced: 10.30   **Time completed:** 11.00 am

Name of child: Mark   **Age:** 8 weeks

Setting: At home during midwifes follow-up visit.

Aim/purpose/focus: To record a baseline for Mark's developmental stages during his first year following a premature birth (32 weeks).

Record of observation
Mark is lying on his back in his cot. His head is in midline with arms outstretched. When lifted out onto changing mat, Mark's head falls back and needs support. His weight is now 3.6 kg.

Midwife lays him on his stomach, and he moves his head round to look at his mother. Mark starts to cry, and mother turns him over and talks to him while redressing. He quietens and concentrates on her face. Brigit pokes her tongue out; Mark stills, concentrates and copies her.

Reflection/analysis
Mark weighs 3.6 kg, which is an average weight for a newborn. He is chronologically eight weeks, but gestationally a newborn, as his expected due date was this week.

When lifted up, he had complete head lag, which according to developmental charts is what is expected in a newborn and would normally have disappeared before eight weeks. However, he is responding to his mother and smiling.

At this stage Mark is still being affected developmentally by his prematurity and is below the midline on a centile chart, but social responses are more advanced.

Second observation

Date: 7 February 2020

Time commenced: 2.15 pm   **Time completed:** 2.50 pm

Age: 6 months

Record of observation
Mark is lying prone on the changing mat. He lifts himself up onto his forearms and looks towards the kitchen when he hears the sounds of food being mixed. He is able to sit up with support and take the mashed vegetables from a spoon. At the moment he is teething and enjoys biting on the spoon. Mark is still only having small amounts of solid food and Brigit gives him a breast milk feed.

After the feed Brigit stands him up on her lap. Mark was able to take his weight and bounce up and down for a short while.

Brigit lays him down on the changing mat on his stomach. He pushes up onto his forearms and looks around, then starts to cry. Brigit turns him onto his back and puts a rattle in his hand, which he holds for a few seconds before dropping it.

Reflection/analysis
Brigit says that Mark started pushing up onto his forearms about a month ago and is now able to stay looking round for a couple of minutes. He

has just started to enjoy bouncing when held up against a solid surface. He does not enjoy staying on his back for long and is not able to hold toys for more than a few seconds. He is very vocal and recognizes familiar sounds.

According to development charts, babies usually start to push up onto forearms around three months. Mark was five months before doing this.

At six months babies are beginning to turn over from front to back and to hold a rattle for a short while. Mark has not reached this stage yet.

Mark is vocalizing; using different sounds, and is able to locate familiar sounds.

It is apparent that Mark's physical development is still being affected by his prematurity, but he is catching up. His language and ability to locate sound are within normal limits.

Mark should continue to be monitored, but his development is not a reason for concern at this time.

Third observation

Date: 5 May 2020

Time commenced: 12.30 pm   **Time completed:** 12.50 pm

Age: 9 months

Record of observation
Mark has just woken from his morning sleep. He is sitting up in the cot calling out. When Brigit enters the room, he stops shouting and lifts his arms to be lifted out.

Brigit lays him on the changing mat and takes off the wet nappy. Mark wriggles and turns over. Brigit turns him over and gives him a toy to hold. Mark looks at it and then puts it in his mouth.

Brigit carries him downstairs and sits him on the floor with some toys. Mark sits quite well and plays with a book, but when he reaches forward for a rattle he falls over and begins to cry to be sat up.

Brigit picks him up. She places him in the chair and gives him a piece of toast. Mark picks it up in his left hand and transfers it over to the right before putting it into his mouth to chew on.

Reflection/analysis

Brigit says that Mark started to roll over six weeks ago (seven and a half months). When he is on his stomach he has progressed to pushing up on hands and knees. He is able to rock back and forward but has not yet been able to crawl.

The observation shows that he is able to sit up by himself when in the cot and vocalize for attention. He sits well unsupported but falls over when he reaches out. He can hold an object and transfer it from hand to hand.

According to developmental milestones: 'At 9 months uses voice deliberately and will shout for attention. Is able to sit unsupported for long periods of time and can lean forward to reach a toy without overbalancing. Moves along the floor by crawling or shuffling. Also pulls to stand and begin to move along the furniture.'

Mark is able to sit for long periods and finger feed, but still falls over when reaching out. He is not yet crawling but is making attempts when on his stomach.

He is using his voice to gain attention.

Mark appears to be making good progress in his language, social and emotional development.

His physical development milestones are still a little behind when compared with his chronological age.

Fourth observation

Date: 6 August 2020

Time commenced: 2.30 pm   **Time completed:** 3.00 pm

Age: First birthday

Record of observation

Mark is sitting on the floor playing with a wrapped parcel. He is trying to remove the paper with a combination of fingers and mouth.

His mum calls to him and Mark looks round to face her, then crawls over and pulls himself up using her skirt to assist. He edges along the settee and grabs a ball. While trying to pick it up, it falls onto the floor and rolls away. Mark drops to the floor and crawls after it.

There is a knock at the door and Mark looks round to see who has come in. When he sees his dad, he squeals with delight and lifts his arms to be picked up. He bounces up and down in dad's arms and says 'da-da-da'.

Brigit moves towards the door and calls to Mark. He stops and turns to look at her.

She asks, 'Do you want a drink?'

'Dink,' he replies.

Brigit goes out and returns with a drink of juice in a feeding cup.

Mark takes it in both hands and drinks

Reflection/analysis

Brigit says that Mark started to crawl when he was ten months and pulled to stand and moved round the furniture two weeks later.

He enjoys feeding himself, using thumb and finger to pick food up.

The observation shows that Mark is now confident when crawling, pulling to stand and moving round the furniture.

When something falls, he watches where it has gone and crawls after it.

He vocalizes and tries to copy speech sounds. He responds to his name and recognizes where sound has come from.

According to developmental milestones, at a year a baby is: 'Usually crawling or bottom shuffling. Is able to pull to stand and walk round the furniture sideways. Picks up small objects using pincer grasp and can use a feeding cup with little assistance.

They babble loudly and may say 2 or 3 words. They respond to their name.

When a toy rolls out of sight they will look in the right direction and follow it.'

Mark has demonstrated that he is now able to complete all the milestones expected at a year.

He was born eight weeks prematurely and had severe breathing problems, which appeared to affect his physical development mainly, but at a year there are no lasting effects.

This observation is a useful tool because it demonstrates clearly the way Mark progressed following the normal pattern of milestones, but at a slower rate. It is interesting though that the period of delay was not uniform across all areas. Possibly nurture has more of an influence on social and emotional development and nature (time in this instance) is required for motor skills to catch up.

This observation completes this chapter, which demonstrated the different methods of carrying out observations and considered their strengths and weaknesses. Hopefully you will have thought about the ways that observations can assist you to give the young children in your care the very best chance to demonstrate their achievements or highlight any areas that require your special attention.

Observations are tools, and the examples are written as a guide. You may not have the time to complete yours in the same way, or using the same medium, but they should give some guide as to the best way to notice children.

The following chapter considers ways that your observations can be used in order to reflect on the ways that children can be helped to progress in their learning or behaviour.

Extending and Utilizing your Observations

4

-
-
-
-
-

By the end of the previous chapter you should have satisfied yourself that the observations you have completed have met three main criteria:

1 You have observed children carefully enough, and for sufficient time, to understand what they are capable of. This may have required observing on more than one occasion or using a different method.

2 You have read widely and understand why children behave in the ways that they do. You have an understanding of the expected developmental stages.

3 You have used the knowledge gained to reflect and make recommendations that encourage children to move forward in their development. These should be challenging enough to enable children to feel a sense of achievement, but are not beyond the child's ability, and where possible are child led.

Once you are well practised in observing you will probably find that you are automatically assessing children throughout the working day. By observing what children are interested in, and what they are trying out, it may give you ideas for future planning.

However, there may be times when you make generalizations about a group, especially larger groups where individual children may be overlooked.

Joan Tough, one of the leading figures in primary education in the 1970s, found that when talking to teachers about their classes, one commented: 'I haven't any quiet ones . . . I wish I had; all my children talk all the time.'

Among those children she later ran a sampling check on, was a child called Sheila. These were the comments she made after the observation:

> Sheila gave an answer when I spoke to her, just a short one, but I
> couldn't tell what she said. I never saw her speak to anyone else and
> much of the time she was on her own, playing with the jigsaws or
> pegboard. In fact, she never moved from the table until playtime. I think
> she needs help trying out other things, and in approaching other
> children. I must find out what her speech difficulties are. *(Tough (1976))*

This observation was undertaken in a reception class in the 1970s and reflects the language used then. Children entered school in the term after they reached 5 and the summer term was the busiest, with the youngest children joining last. Many children had not attended a playgroup and there were no classroom assistants at this time. It could be easy to overlook some children for a while. The sampling observation enabled the teacher to see that Sheila's development was not that expected for the age group in her class.

How to set your level of expectation

You will have learnt from working with children, studying research and using Foundation Stage standards, what you might expect children to be doing at different stages in their development.

This should enable you to work with parents and, if necessary, to suggest a specialist referral if a child is failing to progress as expected. Within the nursery or school setting this would normally be through the SENCO (Special Education Needs Co-ordinator).

For instance, the parent of a child, new to the nursery, is concerned that her 2-year-old son is only using the words 'mum', 'dad' and 'ball'. Her older daughter was using a much wider vocabulary at this age, so should she be worried? The first thing we would need to know is what is expected for the age.

As psychologist Harold Fishbein (1984) noted:

As soon as we can describe a developmental sequence and locate a child on that sequence we can begin to make some reasonable judgments about his rate of development, whether behind or ahead of other children, and to make some predictions as to what to expect next.

It would also be valuable to undertake an observation of your own to see if he is communicating with other children while in nursery. There is a possibility that his sister is doing the talking for him at home. If your observation demonstrates that he is not talking, then you have evidence to refer on.

Language is also important because it is often linked to ability as the child progresses in their education. Much of what children appear to understand is expressed in the language that they use to describe.

Until the child can express his ideas, intentions and needs through the use of language, other people can only guess what it is that he wants them to know from his gestures and actions, from the tone of his voice and facial expression. *(Tough (1976))*

Although this is still to some extent true today, in practice childcare professionals working closely with their group will learn what a lot of the gestures etc. mean. They are able to understand children who are either unwilling, or unable, to communicate their needs verbally. This might also be true for those working with special need children who have a language delay, or children who have English as a second language, and are learning two languages at once.

However, if you are aware of what are considered to be the stages for the development of language, you can reassure parents who feel their child has a difficulty with words.

As Julia Berryman writes: 'Young children by the age of three or four often produce sentences containing the regularized form of irregular words. Examples of this would be: "I digged in the garden", "We holded the kittens", "The sheeps runned away"' (Berryman et al., 2006).

This also raises an interesting question about how children acquire language. It cannot be just by hearing it, as they are unlikely to have heard the sentences in the quote. You might want to read further the theories of linguists such as Noam Chomsky and Julia Falk.

Most importantly, language not only relates to the number of words a child uses, but also to how much a child understands of what is being said.

We cannot gain a true picture of a child's ability unless they have the opportunity to demonstrate what they are capable of. We need to be aware of the cultural, social, emotional, and physical factors that may affect our evaluation.

Indeed, Margaret Donaldson (in Grieve and Hughes, 1990) believes that: 'Failure is a perverse inability of the teacher and student to come to terms with communication problems.'

This is not usually a conscious decision, but as children grow older we begin to rely heavily on an understanding of language, both written and spoken, in order to evaluate progress.

Many people, who did not have their dyslexia recognized and addressed as children, can testify to the trauma this caused in their lives, as they were often seen as less than able when taking exams.

In a discussion on writing, Miranda Jones (in Grieve and Hughes, 1990) comments:

> The importance that society places on literacy and logic means that
> children who find it difficult to learn are quickly made to feel inadequate.
> The teacher's task, therefore, is to build on what the child has already
> discovered about reading and writing. Obviously this will be facilitated by
> knowing what sort of a knowledge base is already in existence.

This is why a thorough assessment using developmental checklists and detailed observation is so important. Observations should become 'records of achievement' with recommendations for targets for further achievement.

Consider the following situation

A mother brings her daughter Amy to your nursery for a visit. The family are newcomers to the area, having recently moved back after living abroad.

Amy has never attended a nursery and her mother is anxious about how she will settle. Amy and her mum stay for an hour, during which time Amy stays close to mum, hiding her head when approached by staff. A further visit follows a similar pattern.

After discussion between the manager and Amy's mother, it is agreed that Amy will attend three mornings a week. When asked if Amy has any special name for 'toilet', 'drink' etc., mother says 'no'.

The next day Amy is brought to the nursery by her father, who explains his wife cannot face seeing Amy possibly upset when left.

Amy will be in your room, so you help her take her coat off and stay with her. When father leaves, saying goodbye, she begins to cry quietly. You introduce her to other children sitting at the puzzle table and stay with her. You start doing one of the puzzles and ask Amy if she would like to help. She does not respond but has stopped crying.

Amy stays close as you show her the various areas available to play in, but she shows little interest. Outside you show her the bikes and prams and she takes hold of a pram, but a child rushes past on a bike so she lets go and clings to your hand.

After hand washing it is time for snack. Amy is offered milk or juice and she points at the juice. Following snack, the children sit to listen to a story. Amy appears to be listening but does not respond to any of the questions. At the end of the session, when mother arrives, she smiles and runs over to her.

A pattern develops over the next sessions. Amy cries initially but soon stops. She will try puzzles and drawing but always stays close to you. She watches other children but makes no attempt to join in. She responds to questions with nods, and if she needs the toilet, she pulls you towards the door. At first you attribute this to Amy being shy. She is an only child and is unused to mixing or being separated from mum. However, as the behaviour continues, you do wonder if there is something wrong.

What should you do?

First raise your concerns with other staff: have they noticed the same pattern of behaviour? Your manager may then ask you to carry out an observation, before discussing the outcome with the parents.

What are your main concerns?

You feel that Amy should be settling in by now and beginning to join in with other children. You have not noticed Amy speaking to anyone, including yourself, who has had the most contact.

How are you going to find out if this is a true picture, remembering that you want to give Amy the best possible chance to demonstrate her abilities?

Activity 1

Look back at the examples given in Chapters 2 and 3 for ways to undertake different observations. Decide which method would give Amy the best opportunity to show her abilities, and what your objectives would be to allow you to make informed decisions.

If your observation, or observations, confirms that Amy is not joining in with other children, and is not speaking to anyone, then you need to consider whether this is what you would expect of a child of her age.

How are you going to do that?

You could compare Amy's behaviour with that of the other children in your room, but you would also need to research the language and social skills expected at 3 years. This would give an objective view of what to base your conclusions on.

The fact that you noticed Amy's behaviour would suggest that she was not behaving like other children of a similar age. *Development Matters* (DfE, 2020) states that the 3- to 4-year-old 'Uses a wide range of vocabulary', and 'Becomes more outgoing with unfamiliar people in in the safe context of the setting'.

You would also need to understand how speech develops, before suggesting any further investigation and action planning.

> **Remember: plan and carry out activity + observation + evaluation = action**

Joan Tough, in *Listening to Children Talking* (1976), has a chapter dealing with 'The child who does not talk'. Although the research was carried out over forty years ago, many of the findings still appear relevant today. Three main reasons for lack of speech are generally accepted: physical impairment (e.g. cleft palate, hearing loss), lack of stimulation, and emotional disturbance.

Joan Tough used extensive observation as an assessment tool, but also commented that it is vital to talk to families to gain a fuller picture of the situation. For instance, for some, there is a familial tendency for children to start talking later.

In this instance it would be very important to arrange an interview with Amy's parents in order to find out if Amy talks at home, and to see if she has had opportunities for mixing with other children. Your manager would arrange the meeting, but you might be asked to attend, as you are Amy's principal carer at the nursery.

At the interview, Amy's father admits that he has not spent a great deal of time with Amy. He works long hours and she is often in bed when he comes home. Amy's mother is a quiet person herself, and when living abroad seldom went out, as she was not confident with the language. She spent a lot of time with Amy, drawing, cooking and playing games, but they did little singing. She did not talk much about what they were doing, as it seemed strange to describe things to your own child. Amy had not been to the local kindergarten as there were no other English-speaking children.

Both parents were happy with Amy's development. She had walked at a year, was toilet trained at eighteen months and seemed to understand when asked to do something. They admitted that she only used the occasional word, relying on the fact that they understood her gestures.

How would you expect your manager to proceed?

It appears that Amy is a much-loved child, but that she may not have been spoken to very often, and she has not had opportunities to socialize with other children. Her physical and cognitive development is within expected limits, and may even be advanced in the detail shown in her drawing.

One possibility could be that she has a degree of hearing loss. The family has been living abroad and a Health Visitor may not have monitored Amy's hearing, vision and development. Amy's mother says that a doctor was available to families through her husband's firm. Amy had received her immunisations but had not had any screening tests. The family is now registered with a GP, so an appointment with the Health Visitor would be a good idea.

If it were found that Amy did have a hearing loss, and no specific cause such as an ear infection was found, the health visitor would probably refer her for a more exact test with an audiologist.

A hearing loss is often the reason why a child fails to talk, but if you have read widely you may have discovered that 'pre-school language impairment, or the late acquisition of speech, are important and useful indicators of dyslexia' (Ott, 1997).

There is also a condition described as 'elective mute' or 'selective mutism', where a child decides not to talk, usually for emotional reasons. There are several other indicators and the speech therapist or educational psychologist will take a careful history before suggesting any diagnosis.

It will not be you, or your manager who will make any of these decisions, but it was your initial observation that led to the matter being investigated. Hopefully there will not be a long-term problem, but the longer any concern is left, the chances of it intensifying are increased.

In the meantime, until these follow-ups take place, there are things you can do to help Amy by planning activities that encourage sounds and speech, making sure that you:

- Look at Amy when you talk.
- Use gestures to reinforce your instructions.
- Name objects as you play with them.
- Encourage interaction in small groups without too much distraction.
- Praise and encourage any attempts to interact with others or make sounds.

You then need to continue to observe and record her achievements. This becomes a planning cycle.

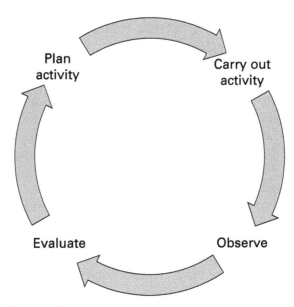

Figure 4.1 Planning cycle.

This cycle is important for all children, Observation is the only way to reflect and evaluate a plan to see if it is succeeding, or if changes are necessary.

The next two observations demonstrate how two children, Colin and Ryan, with apparently similar difficulties – an inability to act in ways socially and emotionally appropriate for their age – actually have very different problems requiring different action plans.

Observation

Colin (3 years, 10 months) used to enjoy coming to nursery, but recently he has become tearful and angry when his mother leaves. He refuses to join in games and throws himself on the floor when asked to take part in the singing or go outside. His spoken language is excellent, his drawing detailed and he recognizes several written words.

It is decided to observe Colin using time sampling for an hour each morning over four days to see if anything is triggering the behaviour.

Record of observation

Day 1

9.00 am: Colin is brought into nursery by his mother. He tugs her back towards the door, shouting 'no, no'. Mother reasons with him and asks him to take his coat off. He pulls it closer to him and continues screaming. His mother is becoming agitated, so a member of staff distracts him and suggests he says goodbye when mother leaves. Colin kicks the Early Years Practitioner (EYP) as she tries to restrain him from running out the door after his mother.

9.10 am: The children are sitting on the mat for registration. Colin sits with the EYP looking at a book. He points to words, asking, 'What does it say?' When asked to be quiet and listen for his name, he throws the book, hitting one of the other children. When asked to say sorry he turns his back.

9.20 am: The children have been asked where they want to work this morning. Colin is sitting in the writing area. He appears absorbed in the activity, and when asked what he is doing, he looks quite indignant before answering, 'I'm writing a letter to my grandma.'

9.30 am: Colin is still in the writing area. He is reading the contents back to himself. He appears to be satisfied with his work and asks for an envelope.

9.40 am: Colin has moved to the book corner. He has arranged several of the soft toys in a row and is reading a story to them. His voice changes as he assumes the different characters in 'Goldilocks and the Three Bears'.

9.50 am: Colin is still in the book corner. The children have been asked to start clearing away, but Colin makes no move to close his book. A child comes over and starts to put the toys back on the shelf. Colin looks up, sees what is happening and shouts, 'No don't do that, they are listening to a story!' When told it is clearing up time, Colin grabs the teddy the other child is holding and attempts to take it back. When

she holds on, he bends over to bite.
(Observation suspended as you intervene.)

Day 2

9.10 am: Registration begins, but Colin is sitting in the book corner. A member of staff sits down with him and tries to encourage him to move closer to the group, but he ignores her. She asks him where he plans to work this morning and he says, 'writing corner'.

9.30 am: Colin is engrossed in writing his story. Two children move into the area, but he ignores them. A child leans across Colin to return a pencil to the pot; he accidently marks Colin's paper. Colin jumps up and shouts, 'you've ruined it'.

He grabs the book and starts to tear it up. The child looks startled and starts to cry. EYP reassures him that it is an accident.

She suggests Colin might like to work in another area. Colin stamps over to the role-play area. He throws the bedding from the cot onto the floor and sits under the table.

9.50 am: Colin is still under the table. Attempts to move him have all failed. It is tidy up time and the children clear up around him. (It has now been decided to ignore Colin, while continuing to observe him.)

10.00 am: Colin has moved from under the table. He goes over to the puzzle table and starts putting the pieces together. The other children are sitting on the mat ready for show-and-tell about what they have been doing.

EYP asks him what he has been doing. Colin says, 'writing a story - but it got ruined'.

Day 3

You are beginning to realize that Colin's outbursts seem to be linked to interruptions when he is absorbed in an activity. He also appears to spend most of the time in nursery on his own.

To find out if this is the case it is decided to observe for a whole morning.

To make the recording easier it is decided to continue time sampling at fifteen-minute intervals but using a chart to record what activity is taking place, and what interactions are occurring

Time	Activity	Interactions
9.15 am	Colin arrives late with mother who explains that he had a temper tantrum	Refusing to talk to anyone
9.30 am	Doing some colouring, being very careful to stay within the lines	Chatting to Early Years Practitioner about a visit to the zoo
9.45 am	Writing about a zoo visit he made with his family	Sitting alone
10.00 am	Sitting on the mat with the other children, recounting his zoo story	Gives full account of what he has been writing
10.15 am	Sitting at a table on his own, having juice and biscuit	None
10.30 am	Children outside. Colin is standing beside the wall. He is scowling and occasionally kicks the wall	Muttering under his breath. No interaction
10.45 am	Takes off coat and hangs it up. Goes over to table and sits with his group. Looks at picture of Three Billy Goats Gruff. Puts his hand up when EYP asks if anyone knows which is the smallest. When picked, he answers, 'This is the smallest, this is the middle sized and this is the biggest. He isn't frightened of the Troll.'	Smiles at nursery nurse. Doesn't look at other children

11.00 am	Colin is drawing his version of the story	Talking to EYP
11.15 am	The children are singing nursery rhymes. Colin is being calmed down after an outburst	Shouting, 'I want to go home'
11.30 am	Sitting listening to a story audiotape on his own	None
11.45 am	Wandering around the nursery while the other children are collecting their work to take home	None
12.00 pm	Collected by mother	Chats to mother about what he has been doing this morning

Colin's mother is aware that he is being observed and is anxious to discuss his difficulty. He does not normally have outbursts at home. He relates well to his two older sisters. A meeting is arranged for the following day.

Day 4
Colin arrives at the nursery in a temper. He is shouting, 'I told you I didn't want to come. I don't want to play; I want to work.'

He and his mother are invited into the office and the manager waits for Colin to calm down. She asks him why he doesn't like coming to nursery anymore. He replies that he doesn't like playing; he wants to do work. When asked, 'What work?', he replies, 'Reading and writing and the computer.'

The manager asks Colin if he would like to go and work on the computer now, and he nods agreement. Colin leaves to go to the computer, allowing the discussion to continue without him listening.

Colin's mother is asked what interests Colin when he is at home. It becomes apparent that he is very involved with language activities and has lots of 'educational' toys. His father spends time helping him play word and number matching games on the computer, and his sisters also encourage him. Being older, they tend to defer to his wishes.

Reflection/analysis/forward planning

When this information is added to the behaviour observed in the nursery, it becomes very apparent that Colin's frustration and outbursts are usually triggered when he is unable to complete a task. It also confirms that he is not very good at socializing with his peer group.

His cognitive development is well advanced, but he is likely to experience problems at school if his difficulty in social and emotional areas is not addressed.

With this knowledge it is possible to plan strategies for home and nursery. At home it might be possible to have a friend to tea or go on an outing with extended family that may have children. Computer games that are played for 'fun' could be introduced alongside the maths and language activities.

Within the nursery Colin will still be encouraged to do the activities he enjoys, but will be warned when only five minutes are left so that he can plan to finish. At the computer he could be encouraged to 'teach' another child. He could be invited to take part in a board game with a member of staff and a couple of other children. Water play using equipment for measuring, comparing etc. could encourage working with another child, and can be very soothing in times of frustration.

Children who are naturally shy or prefer to work on their own will not change dramatically, but they can learn how to cooperate with others, and to experience some of the pleasures of shared activities.

The second observation is of Ryan, who has just had his fourth birthday. Ryan's speech is poor. It is difficult to understand what he is trying to say, and he does not use sentences. He can be very disruptive and often finds himself in trouble. It is decided to shadow him for the morning. This will take up all the time for one member of staff, but it is hoped to discover more about why Ryan has problems with the rest of the group.

Observation

9.00 am   Ryan bursts into the nursery and runs through
           to the coat area. He pulls off his coat and
           throws it towards his peg, but it misses and
           falls on the floor. An EYP reminds him to
           please pick it up, but he has already left. He
           goes into the main nursery and takes a plastic
           giraffe from the shelf that he plays with,
           making it walk along the table.

9.10 am   The EYP is sitting in the book area with the
           rest of Ryan's group, waiting for registration.
           Ryan is invited to join the group, but he
           continues playing with the giraffe. The EYP
           stands up and takes Ryan's hand but he
           struggles and pulls away. He hides under a table
           and begins to chew the giraffe. He is ignored
           initially, and then a member of staff takes the
           giraffe away. He remains sitting and sucking
           his thumb. The group is deciding where they
           want to work first this morning. 'Where are
           you going to choose Ryan?' Without removing
           his thumb, Ryan mumbles something. 'Please
           take your thumb away, I can't hear what you
           are saying.' EYP removes his thumb and Ryan
           says 'blocks'.

9.20 am   Ryan has built a ramp and a walkway using large
           wooden blocks. Another child has assisted him.
           There has been no dialogue, but they appear to
           have agreed where things should go. Another
           child comes over and picks up one of the blocks
           from the walkway. Ryan looks up and runs over,
           shouting 'No, no.' He pushes the child who hastily
           drops the brick. A member of staff tells Ryan
           not to push, as it isn't kind to our friend. Ryan
           proceeds to pile up all the blocks and sit on
           them. Anyone who approaches is scowled at.
           One of the children has told staff that Ryan
           won't let her play. The EYP asks Ryan to share
           but he shakes his head. He races around the
           room, bumping into several children.

9.35 am   The children are putting on their coats to go
           outside. Ryan is persuaded to fasten his jacket
           and runs out to claim one of the bikes. He

pedals well and is able to steer round corners. A child is inside the tunnel, which is being rocked by a member of staff. Ryan gets off the bike and joins him. They giggle together in the tunnel as it is moved.

9.45 am   Ryan leaves the tunnel and walks towards a car. A second child also approaches the car. Ryan starts to climb in, but the other child tugs his coat from behind to pull him away. Ryan turns and hits out at the boy, who starts to cry. Ryan is told to go and sit down until he can behave sensibly. He hunches up on the seat and begins to chew his sleeve.

9.55 am   The children go to wash their hands before snack. Ryan enjoys playing with the water and is reminded to 'hurry up'. He goes through into the area where the tables have been set out with mugs. He chooses a seat, but when a member of staff sits beside him, he turns away, then moves to next seat. A jug of milk is passed round, and the children help themselves to how much they want. Ryan manages to pour some milk that he drinks quickly. He takes a biscuit, and when reminded, manages to say thank you, although he doesn't look directly at the speaker.

10.10 am   The children have been talking about what they did this morning. Ryan remembers that he played with the blocks and on the bike, but only uses single words and gestures.

10.15 am   Ryan and his group are sitting at the table. A member of staff brings a bowl of water and some objects that he places on the table. He explains what they are going to do: to see if they can say which of the objects will sink and which will float when put into the water. Each child is given a turn to choose an object and say if they think it will sink or float. The answers are often guesses but they all have a try, including Ryan. At the end of the session the children decide where they want to go next. Ryan chooses to stay with the water.

10.45 am   Ryan is making quite a mess, so the staff member puts a cloth on the floor and stands the bowl on it. Ryan is happy to sit on the floor and continues to drop objects into the bowl. The staff member decides to record Ryan's ability to predict whether the objects will sink or float. At first Ryan ignores the questions, but eventually he joins in and gets some predictions right. When praised, he smiles.

                 He finishes with the water and goes over to the tray of toys. He chooses the train set box and tips the contents out onto the floor. He starts to join the pieces to make a track. Another child comes over and starts to make a separate line of track. They continue independently. Occasionally Ryan puts a piece of track into his mouth and sucks on it.

11.00 am   The children are warned that they have five minutes more before it is time to clear up. The track now reaches across the floor, and staff and children have been stepping over it. An EYP accidently kicks a piece and Ryan scowls at her. He starts to throw pieces around. When asked to stop and begin clearing up he runs under the table.

11.15 am   A member of staff is sitting next to the table trying to coax Ryan out. When asked if he wants to come out to listen to the story, he shakes his head. Eventually he is persuaded to come out and sit on the mat, but shuffles back away from the group. He is taken aside and asked why he is so cross today. He has his thumb in his mouth and just looks blank.

11.30 am   Ryan is collected by his dad, who asks: 'Have you been good today?'

Reflection/analysis/forward planning
Ryan has good motor skills and is able to engage in imaginative play. His cognitive development is harder to assess because of his speech delay, but his understanding of directions and concepts such as floating and sinking would suggest they are more advanced than spoken language.

Ryan plays alongside children but seldom interacts - parallel play. He does not often make eye contact, and is still putting objects in his mouth, which is indicative of an earlier stage of development.

Ryan is said to have a 'short fuse' and he reacts by throwing, pushing or hitting when he is upset. However, observation showed that he did not always instigate the trouble.

Ryan starts school in six months and is likely to find it difficult coping with the larger groups and fewer adults. He is seeing the speech therapist now and has an appointment for assessment with an educational psychologist. The family is known to social services, who have recently helped them to be rehoused, but they are still in high-rise accommodation with little room for a chance to let off steam.

Forward planning

Ryan has multiple problems and may require learning support in the future, but in the meantime what can you do to assist him? Your observations have highlighted some areas where your support may be able to give Ryan opportunities to cope more effectively, and in more socially acceptable ways.

1 Part of Ryan's problem may be that he has little opportunity to use up physical energy in the flat. He is boisterous, so programme in some physical activities before expecting him to sit and concentrate. It is now recognized that presenting activities outdoors that mirror the indoor activities encourages children's confidence and enables concentration.

2 Discuss with your manager and SENCO the possibility of meeting with the speech therapist in order to plan activities that will encourage clearer speech, as part of the problem is Ryan's inability to be understood by the other children.

3 Encourage Ryan to make more eye contact. This needs to be carefully managed so as not

to appear threatening - maybe looking in mirrors first.

4 Try to distract Ryan when he puts objects into his mouth by finding something interesting to do.

5 As with all children, you should be trying to 'catch him being good', and praising to reinforce the behaviour.

Further recommendations

You will need to continue monitoring Colin and Ryan to evaluate if the programmes have made any improvement to their behaviours. You will also need to work with your nursery team, the parents and other professionals, in order to provide continuity.

The following sections address partnerships with parents and healthcare and education professionals you may work with.

Partnerships with parents

Parents are a valuable resource when assessing a child's development. They know their children intimately and have background information that will impact on how a child works through a variety of experiences and environments.

It makes sense to use this valuable resource, as children often behave in a manner that has a direct link to the home environment.

A key worker is a requirement of the EYFS, and must be appointed to each child before their arrival in the setting. This helps develop the vital relationship between the parents and the setting, especially during the settling in period. The 'key person provides a secure base for the child and the parent' (Bowlby, *Attachment and Loss*, 1998). A secure base makes parents/carers feel reassured, and this encourages them positively to share their knowledge of their child when in the home setting. If children see their parents relaxed with staff they will also be more likely to settle. If trust is established between parents and staff in the early days, the children can only benefit by having their needs met.

Working with parents clarifies expectations for everyone. Good, close, trusting and reciprocal relationships within the setting help parents to manage their expectations, and to be in a position to raise any concerns regarding their child with staff either in an informal chat or more formal meeting. Many family units are often complex, reflecting and evolving within our modern multicultural society. Early Years workers need to value and recognize how parents/carers impact on the child's learning and development. There will always be a variety of styles and levels of parenting, and a great variation in the level of interest shown in children's education. Some parents are concerned about the quality of care and education their child is receiving – maybe not enough 'education' and too much emphasis on 'play' or vice versa. They like to follow their child's progress carefully and to be involved in every aspect of their development and learning. They visit often, volunteer for a variety of tasks, attend meetings and add to information collected for children's profiles.

Other parents are confident in the care given and learning gained. A positive inspection report is sometimes all they need to affirm their faith in the school, and they often only become involved if there is a problem. There are also parents who would like to become more involved, but are overwhelmed or alienated by institutions and schools.

The goal must always be to establish and maintain partnerships with all parents. Opportunities for parents to be more involved should be scheduled for when they can attend. Working parents may need to attend in the evening and may need a crèche facility provided to accommodate other siblings and children.

According to the Qualifications and Curriculum Authority (QCA), one of the key principles of the Foundation Stage is that 'parents and practitioners should work together in an atmosphere of mutual respect within which children can have security and confidence'. There must be good communication between staff, parents and children, where the child's learning is the key factor, and responsibility must be taken to develop positive outcomes for children.

Finding meaningful and appropriate methods of communication to support parents whose first language is not English, and those who experience difficulty with reading, should always be tried. This could include home visits to show photos and routines within the nursery, and inviting parents to come to the nursery to take part in activities demonstrating the learning outcomes. This will help build up a good rapport with these parents and demonstrate the value of positive communication while recognizing the cultural diversity of families.

Where a child has a special educational need, parents and carers usually understand their child's development and individual need best. They have known the child since birth and will have worked with the relevant health care professionals. Alongside the use of observations, parents' wishes and knowledge should always be included when developing 'Individual Education Plans' (IEPs).

Other agencies, parents, teachers and EYPs need to share appropriate information and pastoral care in support of all children. This will avoid any misunderstandings and keep all channels open, making everyone feel they are important in supporting the team.

Pastoral care is especially important for both children and parents. Parents are happy when things are going well but need to know they can rely on staff for support when things are not as satisfactory as they should be. Educational progress is important to all parents and they will benefit from understanding the expectations of the setting, how they can support and encourage their children's learning, and who to go to for help if there is a problem.

Staff need to make sure that the setting has accommodated all family structures; that a diversity of cultural, language and faiths is reflected within the setting and that parents have been involved in discussion about how their child's needs are being met within the National guidelines. To achieve this, staff need to listen to parents and to make planned and active attempts to involve all parents rather than automatically assume a lack of interest.

Some suggestions for how this can be accomplished are:

- Make time to talk to parents and to record information about the child's progress and achievements.

- Take every opportunity to chat informally with parents.

- Some parents require more attention than others, so keep a record of which ones you have spoken to.

- Share observations with parents and encourage them to reinforce the interests of the child at home. Share an online learning journal and encourage them to contribute to their child's journal by adding photos of activities and outings etc. This contact helps build shared knowledge to support the child's development and progress, and provides a comprehensive record of a child's journey through their early years. Parents can view their child's progress in the knowledge that all information held online is securely kept.

- Pass on to other staff information given by parents about any changes at home. Some of this information may be important for the child's welfare, but may not be formally recorded e.g. a family member's absence or illness.

- If possible, provide a room where parents are able to meet for coffee, relax and share experiences with other parents, and where staff can drop in for informal chats.

- Keep parents fully informed about the curriculum with workshops, videos, brochures, displays, social media and online information for those parents who find it difficult to attend school as often as they would like.

- Provide an outline of the term's activities, to which parents may be able to contribute resources, and suggest ideas for displays linked to the area of learning. For example, a common topic in nursery, reception or year 1 is 'Where I live'. Parents who have lived in the local area for a long time may have valuable contributions to make.

- Where possible, on occasion invite parents to stay and watch the children working so that they gain a better understanding of the aims and objectives of the teaching.

- Parent/Teacher associations can involve parents in decisions about the topics and timings of open days, parents' evenings and workshops in order to enable as many as possible to attend.

- Encourage parents to borrow books to share with their children at home.

A nursery/school that builds positive relationships with parents is likely to be able to provide children with a rich environment, which enables them to develop to their full potential. Strong partnerships between practitioners and parents are also a foundation for shared trust, which can only be beneficial to the children.

Professionals you may meet as part of your role

Health service

Family doctor (GP)

General Practitioners (GPs) work in primary care and everybody is entitled to be registered with one. A GP is part of a clinical commissioning group (CCG), having responsibility for buying healthcare from secondary healthcare providers such as hospital and community trusts, and the independent voluntary sector. A doctor (GP) is the first point of contact for most patients, with most of his/her work being undertaken during consultations in the surgery and during home visits. Doctors provide a complete spectrum of care and often deal with problems that combine physical, psychological and social facets. Family doctors work in the community, sometimes alone but more usually as a member of a group practice. They are often based in a Health

Centre with other professionals. Many health centres have Well Person Clinics and Well Baby Clinics run in conjunction with the Health Visitor. The doctor can make referrals to specialists and paramedical services if necessary. A GP has an extensive knowledge of medical conditions and they know how and when to intervene through treatment, or by providing prevention and education programmes to promote the health of their patients.

Health Visitor

Health Visitors work with, and take over from, the community midwife, when the baby is around fourteen days. They are mainly concerned with child development and preventative medicine. They work exclusively in the community and are usually attached to a GP practice. Health Visitors support and educate families and work mainly with the under-5s, but may continue to support families who have children with special needs. Following a baby's birth, they offer advice on feeding, weaning, immunisation and dental health. They routinely screen children for hearing and vision defects, and carry out the two-year development check. They offer parents support and advice on family health and minor illnesses, and are able to support when a mother is suffering from post-natal depression. Health Visitors also work closely with other professionals such as nursery nurses and children's centre workers. Health Visitors are often the first to recognize signs of abuse and neglect in children and know what action needs to be taken to protect them. Health Visitors see parents and families in a variety of settings, a family home, clinics, GP surgeries and Children's Centres.

Physiotherapist

A physiotherapist helps and treats people, including children, with physical problems caused by illness, accident or old age. The majority of physiotherapists work in hospitals, but some work in special schools, development assessment centres, in GP practices and in the community. They assess children's motor development skills, and provide activities and exercise that parents and carers can use to encourage better mobility and co-ordination. This treatment and advice is given in a patient's home, nursing homes, day centres, schools and health centres.

Occupational therapist

Occupational therapy is the assessment and treatment of physical and psychiatric conditions using specific activity and specialist equipment to prevent disability and to promote independence in everyday life. Occupational therapists work with people of all ages, and when treating children they assess the child's practical ability and advise on the most appropriate activities. They work in hospitals, community settings, residential schools, GP practices, clients' homes and development assessment centres.

Speech and language therapist

Speech and language therapists assess and treat speech, language and communication problems in people of all ages to help them to communicate more effectively. A speech therapist may be employed in schools, in hospitals, community health centres and assessment units. They assess a child's speech, tongue and mouth movements, and understanding of language. A child may have difficulty producing and using speech, understanding language, a stammer or a voice problem. They provide exercises and activities both to develop all aspects of children's spoken and receptive communication skills and to encourage language development.

Clinical psychologist

Clinical psychologists aim to reduce psychological distress and promote and enhance psychological wellbeing. They work with people of all ages including children who may be suffering with mental wellbeing issues or physical health. They are usually based in hospitals or health centres. To assess a child, a clinical psychologist may undertake a clinical assessment using a variety of methods including direct observation of behaviour. They assess a child's social and emotional development and are often involved when children are said to have 'behavioural difficulties'. They often work with social services in planning programmes at children's and family centres.

Social services

Social worker

Social workers form relationships with individuals and families to assist them to live more successfully within their local communities by helping them to resolve their problems. Most social workers work in specialist teams such as those concerned with disability, the elderly, and child protection. A social worker not only works with the family concerned but also with the family's friends, other organizations including the police, local authority departments, schools and the probation service. Social workers working with children provide assistance and advice to help keep families together; they work in children's homes and manage adoption and fostering of children. They are normally the prime workers when children are placed on 'at risk' registers or need court orders to protect them. Social workers work for a range of organizations, but the majority work in local authorities, independent organizations and charities. Some may work in a hospital, for a mental health trust or other community-based settings.

Early Help hubs – Family Support Service

Family Support Services are achieved by many support services working together to offer a child or young person or a family 'the right help at the right time'. In some authorities, such as Hampshire, the Early Help model is coordinated through multi-agency hubs across the county. These hubs are coordinated by the Family Support Service (FSS) and include social care, health, children and families, and involve a range of practitioners including GPs and Health Visitors.

Family support workers

Family support workers will usually need a combination of relevant experience and qualifications, and work with social services at family centres (previously day nurseries). An experienced family support worker will help support all families and children under 5 in a family centre. They provide advice, support and guidance to parents to help promote positive care and parenting skills and deal with discipline and behavioural problems of the children within the family centre. The role will include the planning, delivery and evaluation of family centre programmes.

Education

Emotional Health Coordinator

An Emotional Health Coordinator is usually based in an Early Years setting and delivers emotional intervention when necessary. This could mean something different for each coordinator in every setting. When a coordinator in a setting is aware a child's wellbeing is decreased, he or she will aim to encourage the child to foster healthy habits to encourage positive wellbeing, which has been shown to have a clear correlation to the emotional aspect of a child's development. Emotional wellbeing will be monitored from a young age, both by the emotional health coordinator and by observations undertaken by other Early Years educators.

Educational psychologist

Educational psychologists work in a variety of different ways to help with problems experienced by children and young people in education. They are involved in the educational assessment and statementing procedures for children with special educational needs (SEN). They use a battery of tests to try to establish a child's needs in order to prepare a statement. This direct work with children includes assessing their learning and emotional needs using methods such as interviews, observation and test material. They then develop interventions to support the child with the problems they are experiencing. Another part of an educational psychologist's role is to work at a strategic level, carrying out research and advising on educational policy development. They also act as advisors to other professionals working directly with children who have problems affecting their ability to learn.

Inclusion officer

The job of an inclusion officer is to keep children and young people in school wherever possible. A team of inclusion officers, who work closely with schools, analyse data and meet teachers so that they can identify pupils at risk of exclusion and work to pre-empt problems.

Inclusion coordinator (INCO)

The inclusion coordinator is usually a member of a school's senior leadership team. They assist in the collection, analysis and interpretation of relevant national, local and school data, research and inspection evidence to inform policy, practices and target setting where appropriate. An inclusion coordinator understands current legislation, and what this means when working with disabled children, and children with additional needs and their families. Inclusion coordinators develop inclusive practice in their setting.

Ofsted inspector

Ofsted is the Office for Standards in Education, Children's Services and Skills. It reports directly to Parliament. It inspects and regulates services that care for children and young people, and those providing education and skills for learners of all ages. Inspectors are experts in the type of service they inspect and during an inspection in a pre-school, a children's home, a child minder's home, family centre or a nursery they will focus on the quality of the service being provided for the children. An inspector will collect evidence by observing the practice within the setting and by talking to people using the service. An inspector will evaluate the setting objectively and in line with the Ofsted framework and national standards and will base all evaluations on evidence collected. An inspector will judge the quality and standards of the Early Years setting by judging how well the setting meets the needs of the range of children for whom it is provider; the contribution of the setting to the wellbeing of the children and the effectiveness of the leadership and management. No notice of an inspection is given to group providers, unless they are part-time or irregular providers, in which case they will receive a telephone call about five days before an inspection.

Special Educational Needs Co-ordinator (SENCO)

The SENCO, in collaboration with the head teacher and governing body, helps to determine the strategic development of the Special Educational Needs (SEN) policy and provision in the school, in order to raise the educational achievements of children who have special educational needs. SENCOs advise teachers and support staff working with children who have been identified as having a special educational need, and liaise with colleagues in special schools and with parents. They are also responsible for co-ordinating provision for children including the IEP (individual education plan), for keeping the school's SEN register and for working with external agencies.

Special educational needs teacher

A special educational needs (SEN) teacher is specifically employed to work with children who need extra support or require a different programme of education in order to complete their learning successfully. They are qualified teachers with additional training and experience in working with children who have learning difficulties. SEN teachers may work with children who are physically disabled, sensory impaired, have speech and language difficulties such as dyslexia, have a mental disability such as autism, are emotionally vulnerable, have behaviour difficulties, or have a combination of these disabilities. A SEN teacher may also work with talented and gifted children. They may work in special schools or be based in a unit in a mainstream school. There are also peripatetic teachers who visit children in mainstream schools. They may specialize in a particular disorder such as vision or hearing impairment.

Teaching assistant

Teaching assistants work in both special schools and mainstream schools. They can work with individual statemented children, but are also involved with groups of children who are under achieving. They usually work in the classroom under the direction of the teacher, but they also meet regularly with the SENCO to discuss planning. They may be an EYP, or hold a T level in Education and Childcare, or have undertaken in-service training such as the Certificate in Learning Support, but local educational authorities (LEAs) and schools usually decide which qualifications and experience they require. There are different job titles in use by different authorities and schools for this job, such as special needs classroom assistant, learning support assistant, support worker or special needs assistant.

Framework for the Early Years Foundation Stage

The Framework for the Early Years Foundation Stage is mandatory in all Early Years settings. It sets out the standards that schools and Early Years providers must meet to ensure that children are taught, and develop well in Early Years settings from birth to 5 years old. The EYFS was first introduced in 2008. Following a review in 2012, the learning and development requirements were revised to form three prime areas and four specific areas of learning. Also introduced were the three characteristics of effective teaching and learning.

In September 2018 a pilot version of the *Statutory Framework for the Early Years Foundation Stage* (EYFS framework) was trialled in twenty-five schools throughout England, along with new Early Learning Goals (ELGs). Sections 1 and 2 of this EYFS framework set the learning and development requirements and assessment criteria, and includes the educational programmes early years providers are required to follow across the seven areas of learning. It states that all early years practitioners are required to provide rich daily activities in order to support every child's educational development. This new EYFS framework includes the definition of teaching currently included in Ofsted's *Early Years Inspection Handbook*. No teaching approach is recommended but teachers must offer effective teaching in the early years to respond to the age and needs of the children being taught. All the schools taking part gave feedback during the 2018–19 school year. Consultations took place in early 2020 between the participants of the pilot and the Department for Education (DfE). It was decided to keep the Prime and Specific areas of learning – all the areas of learning are interconnected and complement one another. There are no changes proposed to the 'Characteristics of Effective Teaching and Learning', which remain central to the EYFS framework. In July 2020, the DfE published the *Statutory*

Framework for the Early Years Foundation Stage – EYFS Reforms Early Adopter Version. This framework will remain in place for EYFS reforms early adopter schools for one academic year (2020/21) or until *further notice*. Also published in 2020 was new guidance and advice for the EYFS Profile for schools participating in the EYFS reforms early adopter in the academic year 2021.

There are four guiding principles that should shape practice in early settings.

1 Every child is a **unique child**, who is constantly learning and can be resilient, capable, confident and self-assured

2 Children learn to be strong and independent through **positive relationships**

3 Children learn and develop well in **enabling environments with teaching and support from adults**, who respond to their individual interests and needs and help them to build their learning over time. Children benefit from a strong partnership between practitioners and parents and/or carers

4 Importance of **learning and development**. Children develop and learn at different rates. (Statutory Framework for the Early Years Foundation Stage – EYFS Reforms Early Adopter Version *(DfE, July 2020))*

Early Learning Goals are the level of development children should be expected to have attained by the end of the EYFS. They summarize the knowledge, skills and understanding that all young children should have gained by the end of the Reception year. There are seven areas of learning and development that must shape educational programmes in early years settings. All areas of learning and development are important and inter-connected. Three areas are particularly important for building a foundation for igniting children's curiosity and enthusiasm for learning, forming relationships and thriving. These **prime areas** are: 1. Communication and Language 2. Physical Development and 3. Personal, Social and Emotional development. (Statutory Framework for the Early Years Foundation Stage – EYFS Reforms Early Adopter Version *(DfE, July 2020))*

In summary, the Early Learning Goals (ELGs) that are in the *EYFS Reforms Early Adopter Framework* are:

Communication and Language: ELGs: Listening, Attention and Understanding, Speaking.

Physical Development: ELGs: Gross motor skills, Fine motor skills.

Personal, Social and Emotional Development: ELGs: Self-regulation, Managing self, Building relationships.

Literacy: ELGs: Comprehension, Word Reading, Writing.

Mathematics: ELGs: Number, Numerical patterns.

Understanding the World: ELGs: Past and Present, People, Culture and Communities, The Natural World.

Expressive Arts and Design: ELGs: Creating with Materials, Being Imaginative and Expressive.

EARLY LEARNING GOALS – PRIME AREAS OF LEARNING

Communication and Language

ELG: Listening, Attention and Understanding

Children at the expected level of development will:

- Listen attentively and respond to what they hear with relevant questions, comments and actions when being read to and during whole class discussions and small group interactions;
- Make comments about what they have heard and ask questions to clarify their understanding.
- Hold conversation when engaged in back-and-forth exchanges with their teachers and peers.

ELG Speaking

Children at the expected level of development will:

- Participate in small group, class and one to one discussions, offering their own ideas, using recently introduced vocabulary;
- Offer explanations for why things might happen, making use of recently introduced vocabulary from stories, non-fiction, rhymes and poems where appropriate;
- Express their ideas and feelings using full sentences, including use of past, present and future tenses and making use of conjunctions, with modelling and support from their teacher.

Physical Development

ELG Gross Motor Skills

Children at the expected level of development will:

- Negotiate space and obstacles safely, with consideration for themselves and others.
- Demonstrate strength, balance and co-ordination when playing;

- Move energetically, such as running, jumping, dancing, hopping, skipping and climbing.

ELG Fine Motor Skills

Children at the expected level of development will:

- Hold a pencil effectively in preparation for fluent writing – using the tripod grip in almost all cases;
- Use a range of small tools, including scissors, paint brushes and cutlery;
- Begin to show accuracy and care when drawing.

Personal, social and emotional development

ELG Self-Regulation

Children at the expected level of development will:

- Show an understanding of their own feelings and those of others and begin to regulate their behaviour accordingly;
- Set and work towards simple goals, being able to wait for what they want and control their immediate impulses when appropriate;
- Give focused attention to what the teacher says, responding appropriately even when engaged in activity, and show an ability to follow instructions involving several ideas or actions.

ELG Managing Self

Children at the expected level of development will:

- Be confident to try new activities and show independence, resilience and perseverance in the face of challenge;
- Explain the reasons for rules, know right from wrong and try to behave accordingly;
- Manage their own basic hygiene and personal needs, including dressing, going to the toilet and understanding the importance of healthy food choices.

ELG Building Relationships:

Children at the expected level of development will:

- Work and play cooperatively and take turns with others;
- Form positive attachments and friendships with peers;
- Show sensitivities to others' needs.

EARLY LEARNING GOALS – SPECIFIC AREAS OF LEARNING

Literacy

ELG Comprehension:

Children at the expected level of development will:

- Demonstrate understanding of what has been read to them by retelling stories and narratives using their own words and recently introduced vocabulary;
- Anticipate – where appropriate – key events in stories;
- Use and understand recently introduced vocabulary during discussions about stories, non-fiction, rhymes and poems and during role play.

ELG Word Reading

Children at the expected level of development will:

- Say a sound for each letter in the alphabet and at least ten digraphs:
- Read words consistent with their phonic knowledge by sound-blending;
- Read aloud simple sentences and books that are consistent with their phonic knowledge, including some common exception words.

ELG Writing

Children at the expected level of development will:

- Write recognisable letters, most of which are correctly formed;
- Spell words by identifying sounds in them and representing the sounds with a letter or letters;
- Write simple phrases and sentences that can be read by others.

Mathematics

ELG Number:

Children at the expected level of development will:

- Have a deep understanding of number to ten, including the composition of each number;
- Subitise (recognize quantities without counting) up to five;
- Automatically recall (without reference to rhymes, counting or other aids) number bonds up to five (including subtraction facts) and some number bonds to ten, including double facts.

ELG Numerical Patterns

Children at the expected level of development will:

- Verbally count beyond twenty, recognising the pattern of the counting system;
- Compare quantities up to ten in different contexts, recognising when one quantity is greater than, less than or the same as the other quantity;
- Explore and represent patterns within numbers up to ten, including evens and odds, double facts and how quantities can be disturbed equally.

Understanding of the world

ELG Past and Present

Children at the expected level of development will:

- Talk about the lives of the people around them and their roles in society;
- Know some similarities and differences between things in the past and now, drawing on their experiences and what has been read in class;
- Understand the past through settings, characters and events encountered in books read in class and storytelling.

ELG People, Culture and Communities

Childre.n at the expected level of development will:

- Describe their immediate environment using knowledge from observation, discussion, stories, non-fiction texts and maps;
- Know some similarities and differences between different religious and cultural communities in this country, drawing on their experiences and what has been read in class;
- Explain some similarities and differences between life in this country and life in other countries, drawing on knowledge from stories, non-fiction texts and – when appropriate – maps.

ELG The Natural World

Children at the expected level of development will:

- Explore the natural world around them, making observations and drawing pictures of animals and plants;
- Know some similarities and differences between the natural world around them and contrasting environments, drawing on their experiences and what has been read in class;

- Understand some important processes and changes in the natural world around them, including the seasons and changing states of matter.

Expressive arts and design

ELG Creating with materials

Children at the expected level of development will:

- Safely use and explore a variety of materials, tools and techniques, experimenting with colour, design, texture, form and function;
- Share their creations, explaining the process they have used;
- Make use of props and materials when role-playing characters in narratives and stories.

ELG Being Imaginative and Expressive

Children at the expected level of development will:

- Invent, adapt and recount narratives and stories with peers and their teacher;
- Sing a range of well-known nursery rhymes and songs;
- Perform songs, rhymes, poems and stories with others, and – when appropriate – try to move in time with music.

EYFS progress check at 2

The *Statutory Framework for the Early Years Foundation Stage* (DfE, July 2020) states:

> when a child is aged between two and three, practitioners must review their progress, and provide parents and/or carers with a short written summary of their child's development in the prime areas. This progress check must identify the child's strengths, and any areas where the child's progress is less than expected. If there are significant emerging concerns, or an identified special educational need or disability, practitioners should develop a targeted plan to support the child's future learning and development involving parents and/or carers and other professionals as appropriate. Beyond the prime areas, it is for practitioners to decide what the written summary should include, reflecting the development level and needs of the individual child. (EYFS Statutory Framework *(DfE, 2020, p. 18))*

The Early Years Foundation Stage Profile (EYFSP)

In the final term of the year in which the child reaches age five, and no later than 30th June in that term, the EYFS Profile must be completed for each child. The profile provides parents and carers, practitioners and teachers with a well-rounded picture of a child's knowledge, understanding and abilities, their progress against expected levels, and their readiness for Year 1. The Profile must reflect: on going observation; and practitioners should draw on their knowledge and professional judgement of a child to inform discussions with parents and carers, and any other adults whom the teacher, parent or carer judges can offer a useful contribution.

Each child's level of development must be assessed against the early learning goals. Practitioners must indicate whether children are meeting expected levels of development, or if they are exceeding expected levels, or not yet reaching expected levels ('emerging'). This is the EYFS Profile.

Year 1 teachers must be given a copy of the Profile report together with a short commentary on each child's skills and abilities in relation to the three key characteristics of effective learning. These should inform a dialogue between Reception and Year 1 teachers about each child's stage of development and learning needs and assist with the planning of activities in Year 1.

Schools must share the results of the Profile with parents and/or carers, and explain to them when and how they can discuss the Profile with the teacher who completed it. For children attending more than one setting, the school where the child spends most time must complete the Profile. If a child moves to a new school during the academic year, the original school must send their assessment of the child's development against the early learning goals to the relevant school within fifteen days of receiving a request. If a child moves during the summer term, relevant providers must agree which one of them will complete the Profile.

The Profile must be completed for all children, including those with special educational needs and disabilities. Reasonable adjustments to the assessment process for children with special educational needs and disabilities must be made as appropriate. Providers should consider whether they might need to seek special assistance to help with this. Children will have differing levels of skills and abilities across the Profile and it is important that there is a full assessment of all areas of their development, to inform plans for future activities and to identify any additional support. (Statutory Framework for the Early Years Foundation Stage – Early Adopter Version *(DfE, 2020, pp. 19–20))*

Providing Activities to Support Planning within Early Years Environments

5

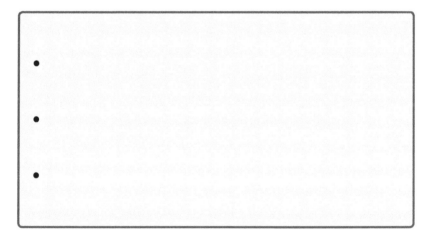

Throughout the book there are references to recommendations for ways the environment can be organized, which will encourage children to experiment and to discover, enabling them to demonstrate their full potential. These recommendations rely on careful observation and reflection to allow informed decisions about the provision made. This should be able to challenge and entertain children, in order to advance their learning and move them forward.

Responsible pedagogy enables each child to demonstrate learning in the fullest sense. It depends on the use of assessment information to plan relevant and motivating learning experiences for each child. Effective assessment can only take place when children have the opportunity to demonstrate their understanding, learning and development in a range of contexts. (2014 EYFS Profile – Handbook *(DfE, 2014, p. 9))*

Children are powerful learners. Every child can make progress in their learning, with the right help. Effective pedagogy is a mix of different approaches. Children learn through play, by adults modelling, by observing each other, and through guided learning and direct teaching [. . .] A well-planned learning environment, indoors and outside, is an important aspect of pedagogy. (Development Matters. *Pedagogy: helping children to learn (DfE, 2020, p. 6))*

As stated in Chapter 1, 'as well as using observations to discover how children are developing and behaving, we can also utilize them in order to plan play areas that enable children to explore freely and express their unique personalities'.

This chapter will discuss how different environments can be organized to allow children the freedom to explore, using all their senses in order to try out their ideas; to learn by their failures and successes, and allow for adult observation so that difficulties can be addressed and learning extended according to need.

Mary Jane Drummond (1998) stresses the importance of observation in order to provide the very best learning environment:

Young children's awesome capacities for learning imposes a massive responsibility on early years educators to support, enrich and extend that learning. Everything we know about children's learning imposes on us an obligation to do whatever we can to foster and develop it: the extent to which we succeed in providing environments in which young children's learning can flourish. We cannot know if the environments we set up and the activities we provide for young children are doing what they should unless we watch carefully, to keep track of the learning as and when it takes place.

These environments will of course differ according to the age of the children. Lilian G. Katz (1998) writes:

Recent insights into children's development suggest that, in principle, the younger the child, the more readily knowledge is acquired through active and interactive processes; conversely, with increasing age children become more able to profit from reactive, passive-receptive pedagogical approaches or instructional processes.

To put this more simply: the younger the child, the more dependent they are on learning through what they experience first hand. They need to see, hear, feel and taste their environment to learn about its properties, referred to by Piaget as the sensori-motor stage, and by more modern educationalists as the period of experiential learning. For example, young children will use a toy vacuum cleaner as they have seen it used by an adult, but are not able to role-play with a group of other children, or imagine it as a hobbyhorse.

Older children are able to pretend and to understand verbal instructions.

Environments vary, for example, from a church hall where all the equipment has to be put out and then put away at the end of the session, to a purpose built nursery where every consideration has been given to structure and layout.

It might appear that a particular building has an advantage, but the main consideration should be the attitude and commitment of staff in providing an environment that will have the welfare and learning of all the children at the centre of their planning. At the end of the day, staff should be considering how each child has made a step forward, however small. Planning for the next day will then come naturally from this, remembering that the best planning comes from observing and seeing what the children have chosen to do. The children will need to feel that what they have enjoyed and shown interest in can be extended when they come back tomorrow. They need to be looking forward to new challenges.

Children also need to feel that they are making a positive contribution to their environment. For example, it only takes a short time at the end of the day to display some of the work undertaken by the children so that they can see it the following day. These displays should be changed frequently to keep up with children's interests. Children could also be encouraged to bring recycling objects from home to be used for art and craft projects, or plastic pots for planting seeds.

The non-statutory guidance materials provided in *Development Matters* in the EYFS has an 'Examples of how to support this' column for each of the areas covered, and the aim of this chapter is to build on that information by giving more detailed suggestions linked to types of play.

We will be looking at different environments and considering ways that they can be arranged in order to provide learning opportunities for different age groups. The emphasis will be on child-centred learning, but this does not just happen by itself. Following observations of the children it should be possible to see how equipment can be presented so that children can continue to experiment and progress. By observing again, we can see if our ideas have succeeded. They may not work out as expected; children may find alternative uses to those planned, but if it is the children's idea then they may benefit more. Staff who show interest in what children are doing, who discuss but do not take over, can also steer the way apparatus and equipment is being used.

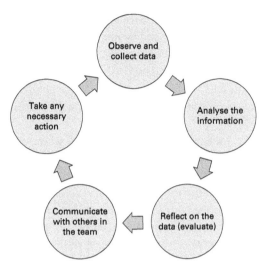

Figure 5.1 Planning wheel.

However, it is important to assess what you are providing now – and how you can change it if needed. Children are active learners and they need to be interested and involved in what they are doing. You can check how the environment is meeting children's needs by following the planning wheel in Figure 5.1.

Some nurseries are run on specific lines, usually related to learning theories of past educationalists such as Maria Montessori, Johann Pestalozzi, Rudolf Steiner and Friedrich Froebel. They require prescribed materials and routines that lead children through stages of learning. Many nurseries use some of the ideas although they are not actually linked to a specific ideology, or they use approaches such as High Scope or the Reggio Emilia philosophy. The concept of Hygge, a Danish approach to life that encourages 'living in the moment' and developing a calm atmosphere where children are comfortable in their surroundings, is also being introduced in some nurseries and schools.

However all these different approaches will still benefit from careful observation and reflection on how each child is progressing.

Activity 1

Find out if any of these approaches influence your current nursery practice or thinking. Research one that you have not studied.

Before considering the different areas within the learning environment in detail it should be mentioned that we also have an obligation to think about ways that your nursery or school can become:

A more eco-friendly and sustainable environment.

Children should be encouraged to grow up with an understanding of how to look after the world that they live in. Eco-schools, a worldwide movement for more sustainable schools, recommends areas where schools can improve and develop their sustainability by considering their use of energy, water, transport, school grounds and waste materials. They encourage an awareness of biodiversity and ways towards healthy living.

One of the most urgent agendas for modern society is global warming and the changes this causes to bio-diversity through extreme weather patterns, water shortages and deforestation. In the twenty-first century many more people are becoming seriously concerned about the environment being created for future generations by the rapid changes that have taken place in the past fifty years. The pace of devastation of our natural resources, the pollution of the oceans, and the air quality will all adversely impact on the children of today.

Many Early Years establishments already conserve resources by using recycled materials, often for financial reasons, and in the past ten years much more thought has been given to considering ways to be eco-friendly and sustainable.

Hopefully this trend will continue and expand, as what our young children learn today will influence generations to come. The Early Years sector therefore has an important role in educating our children, and should dedicate time to thinking critically about ways to include materials and activities that consider the environment.

The nursery or school needs to have on board key people willing to be involved in designing appropriate strategies towards the eco-friendly goal. Much of this work initially will be about daily routines and simple measures that can be taken, like turning lights off and collecting water in butts. Considerations of what materials, and how recycled materials can be used, are highlighted in Table 5.1 at the end of the chapter, but we should always be considering what impact materials may be having on the environment – does the activity promote or damage sustainable targets? We do need to be thinking clearly about materials in use in the nursery. For example, plastic – single use bags, cups, cling film etc. – is obviously not a good idea, but thicker mugs, plates, boxes and toys that can be washed and used over years are best kept until new ones are required in preference to sending them to landfill straight away.

When buying new equipment, be aware of its durability, whether it is ethically produced and whether it has a low carbon footprint. Sustainability can be integrated into all settings, and will enhance the quality of teaching and learning.

An eco-aware, enabling environment ensures that children grow and develop to be resilient and capable across all areas of the EYFS. Teachers in all areas have an important role to play in educating children, and being a good role model when demonstrating ways that the environment can be maintained for future generations.

Creating indoor environments for young children

Role-play

Role-play allows children to practise, imagine and try out their ideas. It encourages interaction and consideration for the needs of others.

Children may begin to role-play anywhere, but many nurseries and reception classes have an area inside that is the focus for themed activities, with equipment linked to a house, shop, hospital etc. However, young children can only role-play with the language and experiences that they know. Themed areas need to have relevance to children's everyday life and reflect their homes. Once children are able to sit and enjoy stories, then role-play areas can also become linked to familiar books; for example a jungle could be the Gruffalo's wood or Elmer's forest.

Children can be encouraged to create their own areas using non-specific equipment such as boxes, sheets, stuffed toys, and differently sized and textured pieces of material. This ability to make one thing stand for another and imagine different scenarios is very important for thought and language development. Children also need time to repeat, practise and rehearse their play as they progress their development.

Role-play in the baby/toddler room

Babies and toddlers do not engage in fantasy play. They make discoveries about their world by exploring and copying what they see older children and adults do. A simple area with objects familiar from home will help children to master new skills. Tables and chairs should be sturdy enough to support babies as they pull to stand and discover the world from a different perspective. All equipment should be washable as babies and young toddlers are still often exploring with their mouths. Large cardboard boxes are useful for crawling in and out of, even if they have not yet become houses. Pots and pans can be banged with a spoon to make satisfying noises before being used to make dinner.

As the babies find their feet and begin to play from the standing position, then chairs can be sat on and cups and saucers prepared for tea. Kitchen equipment such as pots and pans can now be used to prepare lunch. At this stage it is best to have smaller, lighter versions of the equipment, as they are easier to manipulate.

Toddlers are at the stage when they begin to engage in parallel play; that is, they play alongside one another but do not actually involve each other in the activity. They may however use dolls or teddies for pretend feeding. Useful props at this stage are other domestic appliances that children see at home like brooms and hoovers and different sized containers that things can be put in and tipped out of. Simple accessories like hats (washable) and bags are also good for dressing up, with a mirror to admire the result.

It is not necessary to supply everything a young child may need, as around 18 months toddlers are beginning to engage in pretend play, and can use other objects to copy what they see. For instance a plate could become a steering wheel for the car they are pretending to be – making suitable car noises. A wooden block could become a camera or mobile phone. This is a major step, as eventually they will learn to write letters and numbers in their home language, which will stand for amounts and words.

At 2 years children will normally begin using more language in their play, and this will increase rapidly over the coming year. They are now likely to begin describing what they are doing – 'cooking dinner', 'taking baby out'. They are beginning to understand concepts such as size and colour, so tea sets can be used for matching, although if a child is happily engaged in pretend play with the dolls it is best not to interfere and interrupt the flow.

Children are also aware of differences between boys and girls and colour of skin. This does not normally prejudice young children, but can affect self-esteem if they do not see themselves reflected in their surroundings. Nurseries need to consider this carefully when planning layout and equipment.

Around the age of 2 years and 6 months, most children will be ready to start visits to the pre-school room. A familiar member of staff will accompany them and most children adapt well, especially if they have an older sibling there. For a few, however, the extra noise and bustle can be initially unnerving, and returning to the comfort of the familiar home corner setting reassuring.

Role-play in the pre-school and reception class

Aged 3, children are able to play together, involving others in their pretend play that is becoming more prolonged and imaginative. It will depend on space available, but an ideal set up would be to keep the home corner, but have another area that could be arranged as a changing themed space. Most of children's stories start and end at home, whether the outing is to the shop or the moon. Much can be gained from planning to go on the trip and returning safely home.

Much has been written about what to include in a home corner, and we do not intend to include lists here. There are websites and catalogues for that. This chapter considers ways to present enabling environments. The emphasis is on how to present opportunities for children to experience familiar situations, but also to explore fantasy worlds of their own creation.

Home corners for the 3 to 5 year old in nursery and reception still need to have familiar equipment, but now can include real small versions of pots, pans, woks and bowls etc. Another suggestion would be to replace the plastic food with real fruit and vegetables. Under supervision, and with child-friendly knives that have round ends but are able to cut, children are capable of preparing food for a stew or fruit salad. This also provides an opportunity to discuss maths and science concepts. Books, catalogues etc. may also be included in the house. They provide props for pretend play and are easily replaced to maintain interest.

Watching children at this age, you may observe that they enjoy 'secret places'. If your house has a door, which may simply be a piece of cloth, then they can go 'inside' to make their plans. If space is limited, you might consider a teepee. You could then involve the children in choosing what they want to put inside.

The themed area can evolve in many ways. The subjects arising might relate to the season, for example a beach hut in summer or a garden centre in spring. A story may trigger children's interest, encouraging them to act out scenes or imagine new ideas. This is a good opportunity to work with the children to provide the props that they suggest. A supply of boxes of different sizes and large blocks from the construction/loose parts play area can become almost anything. The advantage of cardboard boxes is that the children can use board markers to draw windows, trees, a console for the moon rocket or anything else that they require. Another trigger may be a visit from the fire brigade or the local community police.

As mentioned earlier, the main thing to remember is to try to follow the children's ideas, as this will maintain interest. Knowledge of what is being shown on children's TV could be useful. Occasionally you may decide to surprise the children by changing the theme to spark new ideas. There are certainly lots of catalogues for furniture, fixtures and dressing up clothes, but these are often expensive so thought should still be given to equipment that can be used in several ways. For example, shop front room dividers need not be specific. A plain one means that you can add signs for whatever shop you choose. Shops are particularly useful in reception classes as they provide so many opportunities for mathematical language.

Small world and puppets in the pre-school and reception class

In order to engage in imaginative play, children do not always need to assume different persona. They can use small world equipment and puppets to act out different everyday and pretend activities. This can be seen in the observation of Sophie and her rabbit puppet on page 40–5. They are also an excellent way to provide figures that reflect the make up of the children in the nursery and wider ethnic groups. Figures representing family, characters in different roles such as police, firemen, doctors, builders etc., and fantasy figures such as super heroes, princesses, wizards, pirates, dragons, dinosaurs etc. may all inspire children to invent stories. Farm, zoo and pet animals also provide the opportunity to act out scenarios for children singly or with others.

Dolls houses, forts, castles etc. can all be purchased, but once again boxes and bricks may be utilized. Similarly, socks and paper bags with faces drawn on make excellent puppets, and can provide limitless possibilities.

Small world and puppets can encourage an understanding of the world, its peoples and communities, diversity and rich cultures. It can also provide opportunities to demonstrate children's abilities in the field of expressive arts and design.

Exploratory play

Exploratory play can cover almost anything that children may choose to do. In this instance we will be talking about the use of sand and water, malleable materials and discovery through science, music, cooking and information technology (IT) within the indoor environment.

Sand and water

Sand and water play is messy! Sand and water will end up on the floor, but this should not deter from providing them, especially in the winter months when outside play may be limited. Ideally they will be set up in areas with washable flooring, but if your room is carpeted then there are plastic coverings. Sand and water play provides an opportunity to involve children in clearing up, and providing a specific number of aprons will limit numbers and encourage turn taking.

Sand and water are very sensory, so while they provide many opportunities for maths and science, they can be used by the children to just experience the feel. This provides an opportunity for a soothing and calming experience, which may help children with emotional difficulties like Ben (see pages 64–7).

There is no right way to play with sand and water, but obviously rules covering splashing and throwing will need to be observed.

Sand

Sand can be used in dry and damp form, but when damp is likely to become mouldy sooner. Dry and damp sand have very different properties that may dictate the way that children will play with them. Damp sand will sculpt; so can be used for castles and tunnels with buckets and spades. Plastic figures and lorries can be utilized with ramps, and rakes will make patterns. Using shovels and scoops helps hand–eye coordination and also helps strengthen finger muscles ready to hold pencils for mark making. The landscapes children create encourage imaginative play and working together.

Dry sand provides many opportunities for discovery and mathematical concepts. Because it pours, it is ideal for using with funnels, wheels and different sized containers. Sand play also provides the opportunity for investigation, problem solving, comparing, language skills and working together to share space and materials.

Water

Water can be provided in different sized containers, which may dictate how children will use it. A bowl will hold sufficient for children to be able to wash toys. A landscaped tray with islands may be perfect for imaginative play using boats, figures or fish. Larger, deeper water trays give scope to include equipment that can encourage experimenting with funnels, sieves, sponges and water wheels. Spray bottles and water pistols are best left for use outside on a sunny day.

Older children can experience mathematical concepts of volume, capacity, sinking and floating, and how water can change from flowing to solid when frozen by seeing and talking about it. There are opportunities to work together when holding a funnel and pouring.

Creative materials

Paint is a medium with many uses depending on its texture and the equipment provided. Pre-mixed paint comes in many vibrant colours and can be used straight from the container, but many things can be added to make it different. Thinned slightly and with salt added, it dries with a sparkly effect. When thickened using PVC glue, children can achieve strong textured designs.

Babies and toddlers will be happy to experience the feel of paint and make marks on the paper. Older children begin to plan and take pride in their work. One reason many like to paint on a table is because the paint runs when using an easel.

Paint can be used for printing using hands, combs, cotton reels, car wheels, leaves etc. A simple way to provide a printing activity is to use a paint tray with objects and encourage the children to make patterns, and then cover with a sheet of paper to take a print. Older children might like to design wallpaper for the home corner. Paint can also be used as the background to a collage using different paper textures, cloth, ribbons, wool, string, etc. You can display the work of famous artists in different styles to encourage older children to observe and discuss, for example the 'dotty paintings' of the impressionists.

Other craft ideas might be weaving with paper or wool, sewing and puppet making using papier-mâché, socks or paper bags. These might be encouraged by using puppets for story telling and inviting children to come up with their ideas.

Another way for children to express their creativity is through model making. This could be using recycled materials, as observed on pages 26–8, or malleable materials such as Play-Doh, plasticine and clay. These sensory materials benefit all children but can be especially good for those with physical and emotional difficulties.

You can provide rolling pins and cutters with the plasticine and Play-Doh, but it is also a good idea to just present the materials to be squeezed, kneaded, poked and rolled. This can be a very satisfying sensation and helps improve children's finger and hand muscles. They can also be more creative to produce people, animals and pots, which can involve problem solving to make them stand.

Clay can be messy, although there are cleaner versions available. Some children do not enjoy the feel, but it can provide a good medium for producing work that can be preserved and painted when dry; coil pots an example.

All these creative materials can provide an environment that causes the children to experience a feeling of awe and wonder at what they've achieved.

Discovery opportunities

All play provides opportunities for children to make discoveries. This section discusses how science, music, cooking and IT, within the nursery and classroom, can provide the stimulus for children to make discoveries and develop enquiring minds. STEM disciplines provide a pathway for children to explore a wide range of exciting areas in Science, Technology, Engineering and Mathematics.

Science

The 'discovery' table, ledge, area of the nursery and reception class is usually where science activities and resources are set out. Included could be magnets, circuits, magnifying glasses, prisms, materials of different textures and properties, pots with varying smells and light boxes. Plants and mini-beasts may be brought in from outside for short periods. A suggestion would be to limit the number of items on display at once as children tend to pick up and put down objects without exploring their possibilities if too much is presented.

Staff need to prepare and consider how they would like children to learn from an object – but stay open to the possibility that a child may have their own idea of what they want to do with a magnet. It may be necessary to provide an initial idea for an experiment. Telling a story about a rainy day could lead to a discussion about what material might be best for an umbrella, then the testing out of the children's ideas. Older children may be able to consider ways to record their results.

Growing plants inside means that children can see the results quicker. Beans grown in glass jars can also show their roots for discussion about water. If you provide plants, worms, snails, etc. to examine, this is also a good opportunity to talk about health and hygiene.

Music

Music making and listening provide children with the opportunity to express themselves freely, or to be quiet and thoughtful, considering mindfulness.

Listening to music may aid concentration, but may also inspire children to move in different ways. They can be encouraged to listen and interpret the music in whatever way they want. It is quite simple to compile a list of tunes suggesting slow, fast, stretching high or bending low.

The simplest way to make music is using the voice. From a very young age children enjoy hearing nursery rhymes and later can be encouraged to join in. They are normally eager and able to learn new songs and perform for an audience. Young children are not aware of 'being in tune'; only later becoming self-conscious, saying that they can't sing.

Using instruments to accompany singing or music adds more scope. These may purchased or made by the children to represent their own interest in music such as electric guitars, keyboards and microphones. Older children may learn how to use chime bars, but rhythm instruments such as drums, triangles, tambourines and shakers can be used immediately.

Cooking/nutritional science

Children can be involved from the first stages of cake making; from following the pictorial recipe to enjoying taking one home for tea. Flour may spill and eggshell can end up in the mix, but this is how children learn to control their actions. Making cakes and decorating them is good fun and gives lots of opportunity for maths and science during weighing, stirring and change of state, but not all establishments have an oven or microwave. There are lots of cold cooking activities. Fruit can be used as salads or on skewers as a kebab, where children can choose the fruit that they would like to use. Sandwiches provide an opportunity to practise spreading, not easy for young children, and mathematical language when cutting into halves and quarters. Science language for change of state can be introduced. If you do have an oven available then making biscuits and bread are well within children's abilities.

IT in the foundation stage

Technology has made enormous advances in recent decades and children are being introduced to computers, iPads, games consoles and mobile phones at an increasingly early age. It is important for this to be reflected in the nursery and classroom, but it should be remembered that most of the equipment is used by one child, so little social contact is made. Technology such as ropes and pulleys, tills with a scanner for the shop, telephones and cameras provide children with more opportunity for language when interacting in role-play.

Computers do have a place in the classroom as they provide valuable visual reinforcement when children are learning to match colours and numbers, and they also help fine tune manipulative skills using the mouse and keys.

The EYFS Profile includes technology in 'Understanding the World', and expects that children understand that information can be retrieved from computers, and that they interact with age-appropriate computer software by the age of 3 to 5 years.

However, technology should be a tool, not an end unto itself. One use that has proved beneficial is with children who have a disability where specific programmes are developed to aid progress.

Creating outdoor environments for young children

Benefits of outdoor play

The EYFS framework states that an outdoor environment should be 'a rich and varied environment, which supports children's learning and development. It gives them the confidence to explore and learn in a secure and safe, yet challenging environment' (DfE, 2020).

Outdoor play has a positive impact on children's health and wellbeing; offering unique characteristics and features for learning. Children, given the freedom to explore, are learning in a natural way. They are able to enjoy changes in nature as they occur.

Free flow between in and outdoors is essential, and many indoor activities in all areas of learning can be taken outside. A regular opportunity to spend prolonged time outside in a stimulating environment is beneficial for all ages. Children can become accustomed to a healthy, active lifestyle with opportunities for physical activity and contact with nature. They can enrich their imaginations, nurture their curiosity, problem solve and develop resourcefulness while playing safely and freely.

Modern children lack some of the outdoor freedoms experienced by older generations, with less chance to explore freely, have adventures and take risks.

It is important therefore that schools and nurseries provide a variety of ways for children to experience the challenges of outdoors, remembering that play should be meaningful and child led. The focus of the outdoor environment should be to offer children what the indoor cannot by extending and complementing indoor provision.

Ideally children should be outdoors as much as possible as it offers them the chance to be messy, noisy, energetic and adventurous, to be in control, use their imaginations, and be creative within the natural world. It also allows them to play chase, and to learn to ride a bicycle.

The EYFS document 'Effective Practice: Outdoor Learning' (2007, p. 5) states:

> Children can learn to make decisions, solve problems and grow in confidence in their own abilities outdoors and they need plenty of time to investigate their outdoor environment purposefully. They will make predictions about what will happen based on their previous play experiences and test out these ideas and theories.

Of course the amount of outdoor space available to individual schools and nurseries will vary enormously, but there are elements that should always be strived for. It should be easy to move in and out freely; there should be shelter from strong wind and sunshine; an outside supply of water, and a variety of hard and soft surfaces.

Adults need to be enthusiastic and understanding of the importance of learning opportunities, involving the children in decisions to enable them to become more independent. Best use of space and resources is paramount and need not be expensive. With sustainability in mind, logs and boxes can be very useful. Herbs and vegetables in pots for the children to tend can improve even small areas.

Visits to parks and wild areas are usually available following risk assessment, even in inner cities, and provide an excellent opportunity to study wildlife. They are essential for some pre-schools where outside space is very limited, and the walk is good exercise.

The natural environment

As stated in the opening paragraphs, outdoor play enables children to enjoy the freedom to move freely, but also to come to appreciate nature by actually experiencing it. The percentage of forest schools in Britain is still very small so it is not usually possible to have a woodland as part of the establishment, but many schools and nurseries have some trees and plants or a wild area on the edge of the playing field.

Children connect readily with nature and, if they are given the opportunity, develop a strong connection with the earth and its creatures. They develop a fascination with bugs, being gentle and watching intensely for some time. This gentleness can transfer to dealings with other children and adults.

Being outside gives an opportunity to witness the changing seasons. To see the caterpillars and learn how they will turn into butterflies. To feel the cold and put out food for the birds that no longer have berries to eat. There will be leaves to study as they change colour and texture.

Children of all ages are in contact with a wide range of materials during outdoor play. They can enjoy crawling or rolling on grass, smelling flowers, collecting stones in order to make patterns or transport in a wheelbarrow, dabbling in puddles and looking for worms.

The role of the adult is to observe children and support their needs, to make suggestions if required, but not to take the lead away from the children. There will be times when you want to draw attention to something, to question what their plan is, but always mindful of the need to follow children's interests.

Growing gardens

The ancient idea that gardens can be therapeutic and restorative is still recognized today, and young children are no exception when reaping the benefits. A growing space, however small, allows children to be directly involved with the natural environment.

Planting and caring for seeds allows some children to concentrate better than in the classroom, and may be a useful tool when working with children such as Ben (see pages 64–7) and Ryan (see pages 92–6). When involved with gardening, children can learn how to handle tools, work together, and recognize that plants need the warmth of spring and summer and also water to make them grow. Children can learn about biodegradable pots by making their own from newspaper, cardboard tubes and egg boxes.

Plants can encourage maths skills (How tall are the sunflowers?), creative ideas for painting, drawing and collage, and cooking after harvesting any fruit and vegetables.

Role-play

Margaret McMillan said in 1925 that, 'the best kept classroom and the richest cupboard are roofed only by the sky', suggesting that natural outdoor environments supply much of what children require for learning and development.

The observation of the children role-playing outside at the forest school (see pages 35–9) demonstrates just how many areas of imaginative, collaborative and reasoning abilities were displayed. In this instance the children required no man-made equipment as they had a rich source within the wooded area. Most nursery gardens and school playgrounds are probably less natural, although in recent years the benefits of this are becoming more recognized.

Younger children are less imaginative, and simple outdoor furniture such as a wooden house or teepee can start the process of making it become a castle, fort, shop etc. Sheets are useful for draping over tables, suggesting a den or cave, as children like to 'hide' and plan, just as they do inside. As children develop they can more easily make one thing stand for another – a stick can become a sword to fight the dragon or leaves and stones can be arranged to make the walls of a house. Boxes, poles, tubes, pegs, sheets, blankets and paper can be provided in a simple props box.

Outside areas provide space for a picnic, which the children can have prepared. Lots of adventures can end with a picnic. The area can also become a stage for impromptu singing and drama.

Role-play encourages children to play co-operatively, negotiate and agree rules, and act out stories. It can enhance children's self-esteem and develop leadership skills (see Mason's walkway, pages 30–2). It is always one of the most popular activities that children enjoy; it is allowing children to make sense of the adult world in a child-friendly setting.

Sand play

Children love playing in sand, and the provision outdoors of either a sandpit or a combined sand/water play area gives children the freedom to engage in messy play. A covered sandpit is the best solution for keeping rain and animals out of the damp sand area. Dry sand is best in elevated trays, as it can be taken in but still allows children the freedom to spill.

Sand play materials include buckets and spades, sieves, moulds, spoons, colanders, sticks, sand wheels, watering cans, rakes and combs. Many of these are interchangeable, or can be used in conjunction with the water play area. Children enjoy the varying properties of sand, and it is an important tool for them to absorb maths concepts while they are pouring into different size containers and balancing scales.

Sand helps children to be imaginative and exploratory: younger children content with the feel and pouring into and out; older children devising stories such as burying pebbles and small toys, then searching for treasure. The normally larger outdoor damp sand area allows for extensive castles to be built, combining the talents of more than one child, and requiring the need to share and negotiate.

By continually changing and adding new interest to the area, the Early Years provider can offer a challenging and stimulating environment that improves children's skills across the entire Foundation Stage curriculum.

Water play

Water, one of the basic raw materials available for children's play, is free, fascinating, and encourages curiosity, experimentation and imagination. It holds children's interest, and, as with sand, they are not constrained by needing a right or wrong way to play.

The water play area has infinite possibilities, and when outside the children can dispense with aprons and wear swimwear on warm summer days. Water can be coloured, have bubbles added, and can contain household items such as jugs, sponges and plastic bottles, or hosepipe, guttering and waterwheels. Dolls can be washed, boats floated, and the watering can used to tend to the plants. Fences and hard surfaces can be painted using a large brush, and on sunny days conversations started about why it dries up.

The role of the adult is to supervise, to provide materials and then let the children's imagination do the rest. By observing how the play and discussion are developing, you might add extra equipment. As with sound, water can have a calming effect and some children may just want to pour and watch the droplets.

Water play can cover most skills that children should reach by the end of the EYFS; maths concepts such as full/empty, more/less, heavy/light, same/different, shallow/deep, and positional phrases such as 'pouring through' and 'floating on to'. It also encourages sharing and working together.

Construction play/loose parts play

During construction play children will aim to manipulate materials to produce something new. This may involve building, assembling, stacking, moulding, sorting, and disassembling.

In outside areas there is an opportunity to provide large materials such as tyres, crates, wooden planks and blocks, benches and large cardboard boxes. It is safer to set these out on grass or soft surface as some constructions will be built to climb and walk on, as seen in the observation of the boys building a walkway (see pages 30–2).

Smaller equipment, such as interlocking bricks and toolboxes containing nuts and bolts for joining wooden pieces in order to make longer constructions, can be brought outside on warm days, but children will need to be mindful about loosing small parts. Wooden train track can also be constructed on a grander scale outside.

The role of the adult is to observe in order to maintain safety, and to decide how the children's work can be supported and developed by providing interesting stimuli, but without interrupting the children's plans. The children are learning by trial and error and adults need not make suggestions unless asked.

Construction play provides learning for pre-school children in all the prime and specific areas of the Foundation Stage curriculum. Sharing equipment, turn taking, cooperating, respecting and valuing each other, developing independence, gaining a sense of achievement, and taking responsibility for their own play are key areas of personal and social development.

Children are exercising their bodies and their minds; spatial awareness is being developed as they work out if constructions will work or need adjustments. Size, shape, number, height, length and width need consideration when building.

Giving children the opportunity to discover and develop their own ideas, and to work creatively through this type of play, is a necessary and important part of their development.

Creative play

Creative play includes, and overlaps with, construction and role-play. As these have already been discussed, this section concentrates on the arts, dance and music provision outdoors.

Some art activities can work better outside where there is more space and less need for constraint. The use of clay and large scale painting, drawing and printing can be much freer. The environment is a source of colour and texture that can be utilized to facilitate creativity. This multi-sensory outdoor environment provides opportunities for children to experiment with 2D and 3D materials and techniques exploring colour, shape, texture and pattern.

Different art materials such as water colours, oil crayons, pastels and felt tips can be experimented with while working on large sheets of paper on the ground. Much larger brushes can be used freely. The environment also offers opportunities to observe nature closely and older children may want to draw flowers and make leaf prints.

Hard surfaces enable children to draw on them using chalks or water. Clay is also easier to manage outside, and in warmer weather plasticine becomes more malleable. Opportunities for weaving are also made more diverse by considering natural material like twigs and hemp string to construct a loom, and then using leaves, grass and woody herbs such as rosemary to weave.

Music and movement in the outdoors provides scope for a much bolder interpretation of sound. Most forms of music can take place outside and often this will allow for extra volume; children can sing, play instruments and move in the extra space. There are also natural sounds, birds singing, leaves crunching and wind in the trees and grasses. A performance space could provide the backdrop for acting out stories or devising dance routines.

Children learn how to work as part of a group or independently during creative play. They can express emotions and ideas through art and design, dance and music.

This chapter has considered ways that children can be provided with rich environments that will encourage them to explore and become architects of their own learning, while considering how to provide eco-friendly and sustainable nurseries and schools.

It is not intended to be a definitive list, but to provide thought-provoking suggestions that could be developed in your own workplace.

Table 5.1 gives some suggestions for ways to include eco-friendly materials that can be used when introducing children to the idea of sustainability.

If we want to preserve natural resources, and improve the natural environment for future generations, we need to help children understand the importance of maintaining a balance now.

Table 5.1 Some ways to include eco-friendly materials when introducing children to the idea of sustainability

ROLE-PLAY Small world and puppets	EXPLORATORY PLAY Sand/Water/Creative	DISCOVERY Science/Music/Cooking	OUTDOOR PLAY Natural Environment/ Gardens/Construction
Eco-friendly activities			
Make puppets with clean old socks, using recycled buttons, eco-friendly felt tips, sustainable glue and coloured paper.	Give children the opportunity to collect and measure water in a range of different sized containers, funnels and plastic tubes.	Make eco-bricks using plastic bottles filled with plastic bags. These bricks can then be used for building an igloo or greenhouse.	Growing vegetables, give the children the opportunity to look after the plants and vegetables as well as observing the life cycle of plants at first hand.
Make use of old scarves, pieces of cloth, sheets etc for dressing up, as well as repurposed clothing items. Collect shells, pinecones, pebbles and other natural Items for inside use.	Do floating and sinking activities, discuss the different uses of water – drinking, watering plants and growing food. Encourage children to collect leftover water from drinks and water play and use it to water the garden.	Repurpose small cardboard boxes, tubes, plastic bottles etc. to make musical instruments, craft projects, handy receptacles for storage or for junk modelling. Coconut shells and Gourds can be repurposed into musical instruments.	Pond dipping and river walks – take clipboards, magnifying glasses and a camera to record findings. Was there evidence of plastic found?
Involve children tidying up and cleaning the home corner with green cleaning activities.	Recycle rainwater for watering the plants by installing water butts to which you can add a plastic tube gauge so children can measure the increase or decrease of water.	Source solar energy kits such as fans, lights or solar powered toys, talk about renewable energy (solar and wind). Make kites and fly them, discuss wind energy.	Build a wormery, which will help children's understanding about recycling, sustainability and animal behaviour.

Make pop up puppets of 'The three little pigs' from recycled sustainable paper cups (for bodies) and large wooden beads (for heads). Then tell the story and use real props for bricks, sticks and straw.	Plant willow tree branches (after pruning) to make willow structures such as tunnels or tepees. Modelling clay, where natural dyes from fruit and vegetables are added (but it contains no perfume or parabens) is worth investing in.	Taking children to collect resources for science activities can be a good learning experience. Looking carefully for leaves, twigs, stones, shells, flower petals or pinecones etc. and then using a microscope to look at them in the classroom and talking about what they discover.	Make a bug hotel by repurposing old pieces of wood, palettes, slates and tubing and natural materials such as bamboo canes, pinecones, twigs and bark. Shelter will be provided for a range of invertebrates such as woodlice, beetles, ladybirds, bees and spiders.
Make a mud kitchen, an outdoor pretend play cooking area. Make it from an old toy kitchen, recycled pallets or bits of timber.	Reuse plastic bottles, such as shampoo bottles, squirty soap bottles and small bottles for water play.	Make a musical washing line with old pots and pans. Make a song sack with ten small green bottles.	Use flower presses to dry flowers and identify different types of flowers and ones which are native to the UK.
Sustainable resourcing			
Buy second- hand items whenever possible at charity shops and boot sales for example. If this is not possible, buy new wooden toys and other role-play accessories such as food sets, kitchens and dinner sets from companies that make everything ethically.	Use paper which is chlorine free and certified by the Forest Stewardship Council. Use plastic-free paper tape instead of sticky backed plastic. Buy eco-friendly paint (made from organic fruit and vegetable pigments) and OkoNorm felt tips and pencils made from recycled newspaper.	Think about energy waste sourcing in the classroom. Turn lights off and ensure all plugs are switched off. Recycle batteries.	Recycled plastic is used to make light-weight building blocks and traditional wooden blocks should have an FSC Certificate. Bamboo grows rapidly and is a good choice for sustainable play.

Table 1.1 (Continued)

ROLE-PLAY Small world and puppets	EXPLORATORY PLAY Sand/Water/Creative	DISCOVERY Science/Music/Cooking	OUTDOOR PLAY Natural Environment/ Gardens/Construction
Look for ethically produced products which are durable, have a low carbon footprint and minimize waste.	Avoid microplastics such as glitter and purchase a plant-derived material as its base which will biodegrade.	Laminating makes paper non-biodegradable. Coat paper with beeswax, or press flowers and dry out leaves.	Sustainable outdoor play equipment includes wooden castles, shelters, playhouses.
Tops and lids from milk bottles, fizzy drinks and plastic bottles cannot be recycled but could be used as a collaborative art project. Homemade glue made from water, corn syrup and vinegar and boiled for one minute is a good alternative to using PVA.	Use metal paint trays – upcycled cupcake tins, paint brushes with wooden handles and natural bristles, confetti out of coloured paper punches and hessian (instead of sticky backed plastic) for displaying children's work.	When cooking use local indigenous produce sustainably sourced, organic if possible, have zero waste, be efficient with water and energy usage, avoid using single use plastic and recycle.	Recycled plastic products such as water trays, sand boxes and small equipment to play with can be purchased.
Using time and imagination to resource the home corner means that an outstanding and sustainable area can be produced. By sourcing small items such as little teapots, cutlery, pictures, small wooden tables, fabrics and trays second hand and using real food, the area is attractive and sustainable for the children.	Regularly clean sand and reuse and it can last for years. Although it is reasonably plentiful, digging it up can damage the landscape.	Create a water wall with recycled materials and use containers to collect water at the end so it can be reused. Make kites and fly them whilst discussing renewable energy.	Install a compost bin and a green house in the outdoor area. Encourage children to collect waste and deposit it in the bin. Make a recycled bird feeder. Plan a 'go-green' week each term to include litter pick, bird walk, and energy saving.

Outline of Development from Birth to 6 Years

6

At birth, infants are dependent on an adult to meet their needs for protection, love and food. Their movements are mainly reflex, although the latest research suggest babies can 'copy' certain gestures soon after delivery. They communicate their needs by crying.

Birth to 6 years

The neonate

Physical development: gross motor skills, fine motor skills

Placed prone – the head turns to one side. Supine – the head is on one side and the arm on that side is extended. The Moro reflex, present at birth, will disappear in six to eight weeks. Sight – turns to light and has visual field of 25 to 30 cm. Hearing is acute and smell and taste sensitive. Many reflexes are a response to touch. Sleep patterns vary.

Communication and language: listening, attention, understanding and speaking

Communicates needs by crying, grunts and smiles. Uses movement to explore their senses, turns to sound and shows eagerness.

Personal, social and emotional development: self-regulation, managing self and building relationships

Responds to voice and recognizes mother's or carer's voice when 1 week old. Likes to sleep, but alert when awake.

3 months

Babies are awake for longer periods and are beginning to understand more about themselves and the wider environment. Their actions and language have become more deliberate.

Physical development: gross motor skills, fine motor skills

Head lag decreasing when pulled up to sitting. Kicks vigorously but if held in the standing position, legs tend to sag at the knees. Waves hands symmetrically. In the prone position will lift up onto forearms to look around. Visually alert – follows a moving object. Explores and discovers mouth.

Personal, social and emotional development: self-regulation, managing self and building relationships

Watches main carer and able to focus eyes on an object. Watches own hand closely and plays with fingers. Turns head and eyes to locate a sound and is upset by loud noises. Generally friendly, responding well to main carer. Learning through senses. Enjoys being given attention.

6 months

Babies now have better muscle control and begin to explore more with their hands. Better eye–hand co-ordination allows them to reach out and grasp objects. They are learning that they are separate from their environment.

Physical development: gross motor skills, fine motor skills

When supine they can raise head and lift legs to grasp hold of feet, and when placed prone lift head and chest well off the ground. Can sit with support and turn. Move arms purposefully and when held to stand can support their own weight. Able to roll over from front to back. Picks up toys using the palmer grasp and can pass from hand to hand. Will reach out for a toy when offered one. Visually alert. Still explore everything with the mouth and able to chew and take solids. Uses index finger to point and beginning to finger feed.

Personal, social and emotional development: self-regulation, managing self and building relationships

Wants more company to play with. Usually friendly towards strangers but beginning to be shy or anxious when approached. Most content when near carer or mother. Smiles at own image in mirror, will imitate for effect, e.g. coughing. Beginning to show more independence and developing an individual personality, but still needs main carer.

Literacy: comprehension, word reading and writing

Beginning to enjoy looking at books and other printed material with mother/carer or a familiar person.

Mathematics: number and numerical patterns

Babies' early awareness of shape, space and measure grows from their sensory awareness, the observation of objects, and using movement in play and exploration.

Expressive arts and design: creating with materials, being imaginative and expressive

Babies explore different materials and media as part of exploring their surroundings.

Understanding the world: past and present, culture and communities, the natural world

A baby looks around a room with interest and will scan the environment for any interesting objects or events and will smile when recognizing a toy. They will repeat actions that have an effect, e.g. kicking or hitting a mobile or shaking a rattle.

9 months

Babies at this age are becoming more mobile. Crawling, shuffling, creeping and rolling enable them to extend their world. Finer finger control allows detailed exploration of that world. A child still needs the continuous care of a single most important attachment figure for approximately the first two years of life.

Physical development: gross motor skills, fine motor skills

Shuffling or crawling around the floor and can now pull to stand using furniture to steady. Sits unsupported for long periods and can lean forward. Uses a crude pincer grasp to pick up small objects. Tries to take the spoon when being fed. When exploring shows great determination and curiosity.

Communication and language: listening, attention, understanding and speaking.

Uses voice deliberately and will shout for attention. Babbles tunefully, which reflects speech intonation. Recognizes own name and waves bye-bye with some understanding of meaning. Imitates sounds and converses in a two-way conversation. Search for toys that go out of sight as realizes they still exist.

Personal, social and emotional development: self-regulation, managing self and building relationships

Happy and sociable with familiar adults and children but may be shy of strangers. They have become attached to their families and depend on them for reassurance and show anxiety when left alone. Show interest in everything and extremely interested in their surroundings. May play 'pat-a-cake' or 'peek-a-boo' with known family. Increasingly seeking independence, they will throw themselves backwards and stiffen in annoyance if they cannot do what they want.

Literacy: comprehension, word reading and writing

Is interested in books and other printed material.

Mathematics, number and numerical patterns

Beginning to recognize big things and small things. Enjoys action rhymes and counting songs.

Understanding the world: past and present, culture and communities, the natural world

Surroundings and objects are a great source of interest.

Expressive arts and design: creating with materials, being imaginative and expressive

Babies undertake exploration of media and materials within their surroundings through sensory exploration and using the whole body. Beginning to move to music and listening to rhymes and song.

12 months

The horizontal position of the newborn has now given way to the vertical position of the 1-year-old, struggling to learn to walk. Use of language is growing and they are enthusiastic in experimenting with their limited adult's vocalizations.

Physical development: gross motor skills, fine motor skills

Sits well, usually crawling or bottom shuffling very fast. Pull to standing, using furniture. Walk sideways on tip toe around the furniture (cruising). May stand on own for a few seconds. Picks up small objects with pincer grasp. Can hold a cup and drink with help but unable yet to feed self with a spoon.

Communication and language: listening, attention, understanding and speaking

Babbles loudly, tunefully and incessantly. Understands simple commands, may say two or three words, usually nouns, but understands more. Drops and throws toys, then looks in the correct area when they roll out of sight.

Personal, social and emotional development: self-regulation, managing self and building relationships

Inclined to be shy with strangers and has an increased fear of them, but affectionate to familiar adults. Enjoys an audience and joins in nursery rhymes by clapping hands. Emotionally more stable but growing independence can lead to rage when thwarted.

Literacy: comprehension, word reading and writing

Interested in books and rhymes and begins to have favourites.

Mathematics: number and numerical patterns

Notices changes in number of objects/images or sounds in groups of up to three. Beginning to develop an awareness of number names through number action rhymes and songs. Knows daily routines.

Understanding the world: past and present, culture and communities, the natural world

Begins to be curious about people, enjoys stories about themselves or family members. Looks for dropped objects and tries to find a hidden toy. Enjoys banging two objects.

Expressive arts and design: creating with materials, being imaginative and expressive

Often moves whole body to sounds they enjoy. Imitates and improvises actions they have observed e.g. clapping or waving goodbye.

15 months

The baby is a toddler now. They are usually walking and, although unsteady, are proud of the fact. Their mobility and increasing curiosity make this period an exciting but often frustrating time. Demands on their carer are increased, as toddlers become more daring in their exploration. They must learn self-discipline and adapt to social demands, and this can result in negative behaviour over the next two years.

Physical development: gross motor skills, fine motor skills

Walks alone with feet wide apart, using arms to help balance. Crawls upstairs and can kneel to play with toys. Can push and pull a large truck along but has no control over where it goes. Holds a crayon with palmer grasp and makes a mark on the paper if shown. Holds two building blocks and may put one on top of the other.

Communication and language: listening, attention, understanding and speaking

Jabbers loudly and continuously and sounds are more complex. Can say two to six recognizable words but understands more. Creates personal words. Recognizes familiar songs, rhymes and toys. Realizes that objects still exist even when out of sight. Learning through trial and error – needs to see things happening.

Personal, social and emotional development: self-regulation, managing self and building relationships

Enjoys familiar company, dependant on adults for reassurance. Begins a period of emotional unsteadiness. May become negative and refuse to co-operate or do the opposite if asked. Temper tantrums are not uncommon until the age of 3. Can be defiant, learns 'no'. Curious about everything around, still sees the world from their point of view – egocentric.

Communication and language: listening, attention, understanding and speaking

Interested in books and other written material, especially ones about people or themselves. Enjoys nursery rhymes and songs.

Mathematics: number and numerical patterns

More awareness of number names through action and number songs and rhymes that relate to their experience of numbers.

Understanding the world: past and present, people, culture and communities, the natural world

Learns from pictures and stories about other people. Closely observes what animals, people and cars do.

Expressive arts and design: creating with materials, being imaginative and expressive

Continues to explore a range of materials and media through sensory exploration and the using of the whole body.

18 to 24 months

Children are gaining skill and confidence in movement and gradually adding to their vocabulary and understanding of the world. Emotionally they are still dependent on the main carer and need a lot of affection and reassurance. If they are allowed to be dependent at this stage, they will develop the stability and feeling of self-worth that will enable them to be confident in the future.

Physical development: gross motor skills, fine motor skills

Walks well, can stoop to pick up toys from the floor, pushes and pulls large, wheeled toys but does not steer round obstacles. Can climb onto a chair and then sit down. Uses the tripod grasp when, for example, scribbling. May show more interest in potty. Feeds self with spoon. Developing likes and dislikes in food, but tries new foods and can hold a cup with two hands to drink without much spilling.

Communication and language: listening, attention, understanding and speaking

Chatters continuously whilst playing. Able to use six to thirty words, but understands more and is beginning to put two words together. Enjoys rhymes and singing, can point to several parts of body and copies familiar expressions e.g. all gone. Obeys simple requests e.g. find teddy.

Personal, social and emotional development: self-regulation, managing self and building relationships

Curious and determined to explore the environment, beginning to understand where things belong. Child is still egocentric and refers to themself by name. Plays quite well alone (solitary play) but also plays alongside other children and enjoys their company, but does not play with them. Has an increased fear of strangers, still dependent on familiar adult. Can be defiant and have a temper tantrum.

Literacy: comprehension, word reading and writing

Likes books with pictures of everyday objects in them and helps turn the pages, sometimes several at a time.

Mathematics: number and numerical patterns

Enjoys putting objects into containers and then tipping them out again. Can build a tower of three bricks. Uses blocks to create own structure. Beginning to organize and categorize objects. Undertakes a simple jigsaw.

Understanding the world: past and present, people, culture and communities, the natural world

Remains curious about people. Explores objects. Can anticipate repeated sounds, sights and actions.

Expressive arts and design: creating with materials, being imaginative and expressive

Begins to move to music, listens to or joins in rhymes and songs. Interested in the effects of using a crayon on paper. Pretends that one object represents another, especially when objects have characteristics in common.

2 years

At 2 years old children take an enormous step in their understanding of their environment. They are learning to construct simple sentences that will be the basis on which they will develop verbal fluency in their third and fourth years. The child is still very curious, restless, and enjoys a great deal of physical activity, but may be able to sustain short periods of concentrated effort on an activity.

Physical development: gross motor skills, fine motor skills

Runs safely on whole foot, loves to climb, squat, push and pull large wheeled toys in the right direction. Can throw a ball and kick a ball. Uses tripod grasp to hold pencil and scribbles circles and dots. Able to sit on a tricycle, but uses feet not pedals. Spoon feeds and drinks efficiently. Usually, can control bowels and may be dry in daytime. May have all infant teeth.

Communication and language: listening, attention, understanding and speaking

Uses 150 words and understands many more. Can form a phrase with two or more words (telegraphic speech). Listens with interest to talk going on around them. Refers to self by name, talks continually during play. Rapid increase in vocabulary. Follows instructions. Identifies action words, beginning to ask simple questions.

Personal, social and emotional development: self-regulation, managing self and building relationships

Curious about surroundings but does not understand common dangers. Impatient and egocentric. Still not playing with other children, only alongside them. Unable to share playthings or the adult's attention and clings on to own possessions with determination. Sometimes can be frustrated when not able to express themself. Can be loving one minute and biting the next.

Literacy: comprehension, word reading and writing

Enjoys picture books, turns pages more slowly. Repeats words or phrases from known stories. Joins in with rhymes and songs.

Mathematics: number and numeral patterns

Can build a tower of six or seven blocks. Randomly says counting words. Is able to respond to such questions as please give me one cup? Please give me two dolls? Enjoys filling and emptying containers.

Understanding the natural world: past and present, people, culture and communities, the natural world

Beginning to understand the immediate family. Remembers where objects belong. Can match parts of objects that can fit together, e.g. a lid on a teapot. Interested in toys with buttons and flaps.

Expressive arts and design: creating materials, being imaginative and expressive.

Joins in simple role-play and favourite songs.

2½ years

At 2½ the child is poised between dependence on a familiar adult and the ability to broaden horizons and spend time with other adults and children at a pre-school/nursery. Physically quite proficient, and able to be understood verbally for most of the time. They often still need the security of a familiar environment and should not be pushed too soon.

Physical development; gross motor skills, fine motor skills

Locomotor skills improving, walks upstairs and downstairs easily using two feet to a step. Stands on tip toe and can jump with both feet together. Runs well, climbs apparatus, throws and kicks a ball. Eats skilfully, uses a toilet and is usually dry in day and maybe at night. Shows a preference for dominant hand. Able to control hammers and mark-making tools more deliberately.

Communication and language: listening, attention, understanding and speaking

Uses 200 or more recognizable words. Continually asking 'what and who' questions. Says a few nursery rhymes, concentrates when having a story, sentences still use telegraph speech. Recognizes and responds to familiar sounds. Understands complex sentences. Shares feelings, thoughts and experiences by language.

Personal, social and emotional development: self-regulation, managing self and building relationships

Is still egocentric but watches other children play, sometimes joining in. Seeks out others to share experiences. Still dependent on an adult and can throw tantrums when thwarted. Expresses own preference and interests and own feelings. Knows full name and recognizes self in photographs. More sustained role-play.

Literacy: comprehension, word reading and writing

Enjoys picture books, especially the minutia. Able to fill in missing words or phrases in a story, rhyme or game. Knows a few rhymes. Holds a thick pencil and can copy a horizontal line and circle.

Mathematics: number and numerical patterns

Builds a tower of seven plus bricks, can recite some number names in the correct order, beginning to make comparisons between quantities and to notice shapes and patterns in pictures. Beginning to use some mathematical language such as 'more', 'a lot'. Beginning to categorize objects according to properties, e.g. colour.

Understanding the world: past and present, people, culture and communities, the natural world

Imitates everyday actions in pretend play with happenings from own family and own cultural background, e.g. making a cup of tea. Beginning to make own friends. Enjoys playing meaningfully with small toys, e.g. farm animals, trains.

Expressive arts and design: creating with materials, being imaginative and expressive

Interested in the way musical instruments sound. Experiments with crayons, mark makers and paint.

3 years

The 3-year-old is more agile and co-ordinated. Language is becoming an increasingly important tool. Its social use is developing, and if language development is delayed the child may find it difficult to make friends, join in group activities, or obey fairly complicated instructions from an adult. All these things are necessary when a child begins to move out of the family circle and start pre-school/nursery, which is usually at this age. If the child is not able to use or understand language then anti-social behaviour may persist and ways should be planned to enable the child to communicate in any way they are able to, e.g. gestures, sign.

Physical development: gross motor skills, fine motor skills

Uses climbing frames confidently, can stand on one leg and walk on tiptoe. Steers round obstacles and corners while running or pushing toys. Walks upstairs with alternative feet but still uses two feet to the stair coming down. Moves freely and with confidence whilst running, jumping, skipping or hopping. With practice can ride a tricycle or bicycle with stabilizers, kick a ball and cut with scissors. Is able to follow directions.

Communication and language: listening, attention, understanding and speaking

Extensive vocabulary, usually intelligible to strangers. Asks many questions – who, why, what and where? Speech is beginning to gain interest by changes of tone in a sentence.

Listens to others one-to-one or in a small group. Is able to follow directions. Understands use of objects, e.g. what do we use to cut things with?

Personal, social and emotional development: self – regulation, managing self and building relationships

Show appreciation of differences between present and past and the need to wait for attention, but still has difficulty understanding the need to take turns. More co-operative and likes to help adults. Beginning to join in games with other children, enjoys sharing experiences at family mealtime. Emotional security shows friendliness, sociability and a desire to please. Feels more secure but sometimes develops fears. Can select activities and resources with help.

Literacy: comprehension, word reading and writing

Listens quietly and attentively to stories. Knows several rhymes and songs. Starting to understand the way stories are structured, how a story may end and begins to predict what might happen next. Ascribes meaning to marks seen in different places. Copies O, V and T shapes.

Mathematics: number and numerical patterns

Can build a tower of nine bricks and can copy a bridge made with them. Can count up to ten or more but has little appreciation of actual quantity beyond three. Uses some number names and number language and uses some numbers accurately in play. Shows an interest in shape and space by playing with shapes or building with objects.

Understanding the world: past and present, people, culture and communities, the natural world

Beginning to learn that their friends have similarities and differences that connect them and distinguish them from others. Shows interest in the lives of people known to them. Remembers events in their own experience and can describe them. Asks questions about the environment and natural world. Knows how to operate simple equipment. Beginning to use technical equipment such as computers or iPad if allowed.

Expressive arts and design: creating with materials, being imaginative and expressive

Can name two or three colours, enjoys painting, draws a person with a head and usually one or two features. Plays imaginative games and make-believe people. Enjoys dancing and ring games and can create movement to music.

4 years

After the period of emotional developmental stability around 3 years, children are again showing a 'see-saw' pattern of behaviour at the age of 4. In struggling for the verbal, social and emotional confidence of the 5-year-old, the 4-year-old can become a 'boastful, dogmatic and bossy show off'. Their minds are lively, their imaginations vivid and their will strong, but their emotional unsteadiness shows itself in verbal impertinence and exaggeration.

Physical development: gross motor skills, fine motor skills

Show agility when running, hopping, walking on tiptoe, climbing trees and ladders. Good sense of balance and climbs and descends stairs confidently. Good tricycle rider, and increased skill in ball games. Good pencil control, able to form recognized shapes and letters and able to thread small beads on a string. Capable of washing and drying hands and dressing and undressing self.

Communication and language: listening, attention, understanding and speaking

Intelligible speech and grammar usually correct. Continues to ask 'why', 'when' and 'how'. New words are learnt quickly, longer sentences, and language is used to recall past experiences and recall and recount recent events.

Personal, social and emotional development: self-regulation, managing self and building relationships

Likes the companionship of other children and adults but alternates between co-operation and conflict; however, understands the need to use words rather than fists.

Aware of boundaries. Able to share and take turns but may cheat in order to win. Initiates conversations and listens to others, shows sympathy to a friend who is hurt. Is in a period of emotional unsteadiness, which is shown by being cheeky and impertinent rather than temper tantrums. Has a developing sense of humour. Enjoys dramatic make-believe play for long periods.

Literacy: comprehension, word reading and writing

Can describe main story settings, events and principal characters. Enjoys the illustrations and print in a book. Independently looks at books, takes care of the book and holds it the correct way to turn pages carefully. Copies cross, square and V, H, T and O shapes.

Mathematics: number and numerical patterns

Builds tower of ten plus bricks and bridges. Counts by rote up to twenty or more and may have an understanding of number to four or five. Recognizes and can name circle, square and triangle. Is beginning to use fingers, marks on paper or pictures to represent numbers. Sometimes matches numeral and quantity correctly. Is developing an interest in number problems. Is interested in shape in a sustained construction activity and is able to talk about shapes of everyday objects.

Understanding the world: past and present, people, culture and communities, the natural world

Shows interest in different occupations and ways of life. Able to talk about why things happen and how they work. Shows care and concern about living things in the environment. Beginning an understanding of growth, decay and changes. Shows an interest in mechanical toys. Knows that information can be retrieved from computers.

Expressive arts and design: creating with materials, being imaginative and expressive

Can draw a recognizable house and a person with a head, maybe trunk, legs and arms. Matches and names four colours correctly. Can sustain dramatic make-believe play for long periods of time, often based on own first-hand experiences. Uses resources and props. Captures experiences and responses with a range of media, such as words, dance, music and paint.

5 years

If raised in a supportive and stimulating environment, 5-year-olds are confident and have good self-control. Home will no longer satisfy their curiosity and desire for knowledge, and they are ready for the wider experience of school. Having achieved a measure of independence they are able to cope with the larger group and no longer require so much adult attention – although they will always thrive on praise and be proud of their achievements.

Physical development: gross motor skills, fine motor skills

Movements precise; runs lightly on toes, can walk along a narrow line, skilful in climbing, swinging and sliding, good co-ordination, good spatial awareness and is confident when using balancing and climbing apparatus. Has good control of pencils, crayons and paint brushes. Well-developed IT skills – video, computer, iPad. Shows preference for dominant hand, handles tools, objects, construction and malleable materials safely and with good control. Beginning to understand safety measures.

Communication and language: listening, attention, understanding and speaking

Speech fluent and grammatically correct. Enjoys new words and learns songs quickly. Wants to know the meaning of new words, tells long stories and asks many questions. Maintains attention, concentrates and sits quietly during an activity. Listens and responds to other people's ideas. Uses language to imagine and recreate roles and experiences whilst playing.

Personal, social and emotional development: self-regulation, managing self and building relationships

Ready to mix with a wider group and to choose friends. Co-operative with friends and understands that there is a need for rules. Plays in larger groups of children but often has one special friend. Understands social rules, takes steps to resolve conflicts with other children. Usually sensible and controlled, more stable and emotionally secure.

Literacy: comprehension, word reading and writing

Loves to be read or told stories, which are often used later in complicated dramatic play. Hears and says the initial sound in words, can segment the sounds in simple words and blend them together. Links sounds to letters and is able to name and make the sounds of the letters of the alphabet. Begins to read words and simple sentences. Uses a lot of vocabulary, writes own name and other things such as labels, attempts to write short sentences.

Mathematics: number and numerical patterns

Gaining a concept of number and begins to classify objects. Counts fingers on one hand with the index finger of the other. Recognizes one to five, can count up to four objects by saying one number name for each item, counts objects to ten and beginning to count beyond ten. Can name and draw circle, square, rectangle and triangle. Uses everyday language related to time and realizes that clock time has a relationship to the daily routine of events. Uses mathematical language for 'solid' 3D shapes and 'flat' 2D shapes and can describe shapes in mathematical terms. Can order two or three items by length, height or capacity. Beginning to have an understanding of money.

Understanding the world: past and present, people, culture and communities, the natural world

Enjoys joining in with family customs and routines. Shows a sensitivity and concern for living things in the environment. Completes a simple programme on a computer and uses hardware to interact with age-appropriate computer software.

Expressive arts and design: creating with materials, being imaginative and expressive

Draws recognizable people with head, trunk, features, arms and legs. Creates pictures. Decides what to draw before starting. Capable of colouring neatly and staying within the line. Can name at least four colours and explores mixing colours. Experiments with different textures, explores sounds of musical instruments, plans and constructs with a purpose in mind and uses tools and techniques confidently and to good effect. Plays alongside other children who are engaged in the same theme, may act out a story.

6 years

Physically children continue to mature and refine their control of movement. Growth rates slow down. Emotionally children are entering another period of upheaval. Between the ages of 5 and 7 there is a major change in the way children think and feel and the 6-year-old may experience difficulties in maintaining balance in their emotional behaviour. There are often swings of mood, periods of frenzied activity, and nightmares are not unusual. However, interesting children in new ideas and objects and encouraging them to explore and learn can harness these energies. Independence in reading and writing is growing, and the forming of new mathematical concepts of weight, size, distance and shape are beginning. Six-year-olds are curious, interested and inventive.

Physical development: gross motor skills, fine motor skills

Body is well co-ordinated, agile and strong. They are confident when jumping off gym apparatus, and climb and balance well and can ride a two-wheeled bicycle without stabilizers. Hand and eye co-ordination work well together, they play bat and ball games confidently. Girls and boys are equally boisterous with their energies often being channelled into cartwheels, dance or wrestling. Fine motor skills are good, hold pencils like adults and their writing becomes more precise. They are able to thread a needle and sew, confidently use a knife and fork, and can use tools with good effect using dominant hand. Skills are well developed when using an iPad, computer, video or other digital technology. Understands the need for safety when attempting new challenges.

Communication and language: listening, attention, understanding and speaking

Is an incessant chatterer, so enjoys oral work, but language now widens to include reading, writing and listening. Listens attentively when adults read stories, can anticipate happenings in the story and respond well to comments and questions. Books do not necessarily need pictures, 6-year-olds can distinguish between reality and fantasy and they have a good sense of humour. They talk fluently and can remember stories and rhymes. Reading and writing skills are developing, but they are not yet reading independently and with confidence. Although writing skills are developing, they may still reverse some letters. They use more complex sentences to link thoughts whilst speaking. Vocabulary is greatly extended; their mind is very active and a child will move on from one activity to another.

Personal, social and emotional development: self-regulation, managing self and building relationships

Often initiate conversations, they listen to what others are saying, and they take turns. They show sensitivity to other children's needs and feelings. They can organize activities and resolve conflicts, and their friendships form and dissolve rapidly. They are eager for praise and recognition and would always like to win. They are aware of acceptable behaviour and are more confident and independent, but 6-year-olds are still dependent on adults for direction and guidance.

Literacy: comprehension, word reading and writing

Vocabulary increases by five to ten new words every day and can recognize more than 200 sight words. Most sound patterns are established. Different ways are used to help read and understand a story, e.g. by asking questions, by predicting what is going to happen and by visual clues and self-correcting by re-reading when a mistake is made. Verbalize out loud sounds in a word when trying to spell. Beginning to understand the past, present and future. The pencil is held with a dynamic tripod grasp. Beginning to use punctuation and capital letters and developing improved handwriting by added spaces between words. The written word is becoming more advanced.

Mathematics: number and numerical patterns

Able to write and recognize numerals from 0 to 100, and able to say which number is one more or one less than a given number. Are able to solve problems including doubling, halving and sharing, can read and write number words from zero to twenty, can count to 100 by ones, twos, fives, and tens, and count backwards from ten. Are able to compare, order and represent numbers to fifty using objects, do basic addition and subtraction up to twenty, and mentally add together single digit numbers. Begin to develop concepts of measurement, distance, length, volume, capacity, time and area. Able to recognize and know the value of money up to £1. Know the differences between circles, square, triangle and rectangle. Read and create a simple bar graph and record data on a chart.

Understanding the world: past and present, people, culture and communities, the natural world

Can talk about past and present events. Are becoming more aware of the influence of cultural conventions in writing and drawing. Are interested in animals and plants with observations enhancing this. Morals and values are developing. Children are more aware of events like natural disasters, other cultures and lifestyles, different weather patterns and the preservation of the earth, all of which they can view on the television. Many 6-year-olds have access to computers in and outside of school. Children's attitude to technology is usually positive and many 6-year-olds have a good understanding of digital technology.

Expressive arts and design: creating with materials, being imaginative and expressive

Children are eager, creative, curious and adept, they are highly motivated and still retain fantasy in their play. They enjoy experimentation with different media. They are often self-critical of their own work and are concerned how others may view their work. Fun activities such as acting out stories using simple home-made props, making and using puppets and singing songs help learning and development. Children are expressing themselves, exploring ideas and solving problems. Art and craft activities help the children to communicate feelings, ideas and messages. Children gain enjoyment from experimenting with musical concepts, such as volume, rhythm, tempo and pitch.

Theoretical perspectives on children's development

Observation of children is used as a systematic tool in studying children and their developing skills. *Development Matters* (DfE, 2021), written by Dr Julian Grenier for Early Years practitioners, is a guide for their professional judgement of how children develop and learn. He emphasizes how important it is to understand 'A child's interest, who they are as an individual, their difficulties and obstacles and when they might need extra help. Practitioners should be carefully noticing and listening'. Grenier has used 'noticing' rather than observing in *Development Matters*. This reflects that the new changes should not mean an onerous data gathering process. 'Noticing' is not another word for observation, but a starting point for the process of observing, which should make observing a slower, deliberate, reflective and analytical process. Observations need not necessarily be long and time consuming, they are helpful for practitioners to understand the needs of a child and give them a small insight into a child's development. Many observations are 'in the moment' as practitioners notice carefully what the child/children are doing, and they respond immediately. Learning journeys are special moments of something new, for example playing with a new friend, which when recorded helps over time to tell the child's progress.

Development Matters gives guidance for observation checkpoints for the prime areas and will help prompt practitioners to be aware of areas where children may need additional support.

In this chapter *Development Matters* is going to be the main reference for child development. There are several quotes from it and thereafter some activities for consolidation of various areas of child development. The other aspect of this chapter is to familiarize readers with some well-known theorists. Following, are examples of activities that you can undertake in order to consolidate your knowledge of theorists' perspectives.

Here are examples of some ways to support the development of a child between 0 and 3 years in the prime area of Communication and Language, understanding that:

- Babies love singing and music, action rhymes and games.
- Babies respond to familiar voices.
- Babies take turns, babble and use single words.
- Babies can listen and respond to simple instruction.

Activity 1

Research further activities that would support the communication of children aged 0 to 3 years.

Research information that will give you a clear understanding of how young children vary in their language development.

Name a theorist whose work involved studying babies aged 0–18 months, and write briefly about their theory of the acquisition of language.

The following example is of how a 3- to 4-year-old can be supported as part of the prime area of Communication and Language:

- Provide a rich language environment by sharing books throughout a session and offer at least one daily story time.
- Extend children's vocabulary, giving explanations to help to make sure that children understand.
- Offer children lots of interesting objects to investigate some of which incorporate the child's own interest.

Activity 2

Research further activities that would support the communication of children aged 3 to 4 years.

How can the environment be language rich? Make suggestions, and explain how the children would gain new vocabulary from undertaking this activity.

Research a theorist who has studied language development in young children, and give an outline of their ideas.

This example covers how a 3- to 4-year-old can be supported as part of the prime area of Literacy. They are learning how to write some letters, and physical skills are needed in order to write letters accurately, so:

- Give practice to improve small muscle co-ordination.
- Large muscle movement co-ordination should also to be practised.
- Learn the language of direction, up, down, back, round.

Activity 3

Give detailed examples of how to support children learning to form letters. Make sure you give examples of activities linked to physical skills and language development.

Research the language of direction, give the reasons as to why this is important for children to learn in order to write letters accurately.

Reflect on activities linked to physical skills and why they are important. Give detailed examples of these activities.

This example describes how children in a reception class can be supported as part of the prime area of literacy. They are learning how to form lower case and capital letters correctly.

- Make books available to all children.
- Encourage children to learn the formation of letters alongside learning the sounds for each letter.
- Use memorable phrases for each letter.

Activity 4

Research different methods of teaching letter formation as the children learn the sounds for each letter.

Observe a group of children and their teacher in a reception class. Find out how the teacher applies her methods to encourage the school's phonic programme.

Children who are left-handed need practitioners to use simple strategies to enable them to achieve success. Consider classroom management and recommend writing materials and implements when working with children who are left-handed, e.g. model letter formation, sky writing specifically for children who are left-handed with your left hand.

Theorists

There is no one theory or theorist that encompasses all areas of child development. However, child development theories and theorists have influenced early years practice over many years. Theorists and educators often used observations of their own children as some of them came from diverse backgrounds and disciplines. They were also interested in how children acquired knowledge and learnt.

In order to gain a better knowledge of child development, many theories have evolved over time. This interest largely developed in the early twentieth century. Prior to then, children were viewed as small versions of adults and not a lot of attention was given to their growing up. In the twenty-first century, many more theorists, present and past, are influencing the thinking on child development, Early Years practice and in the writing of guidelines for the Early Years sector. *Development Matters*, the Early Years Foundation Stage (EYFS) and *Birth to 5 Matters* all contain the influence, in some form or other, of some theories and theorists.

The following quotations are from 'Theories of Development: How They Have Influenced the EYFS', published by Early Years Guidance, 2020.

Humanist theory (Maslow)

The hierarchy of needs is common to all human beings. The hierarchy demonstrates that basic needs must be met before children are able to focus on learning. It states that each child is unique. It encourages you to think about how you observe individual children to see how they play, and be able to meet their individual interests in the present moment, encouraging a natural instinct to learn, explore and question. Getting to know the child is important; how they choose to do things and allowing for child-initiated play.

Where do you see this theory within the EYFS?
The EYFS states that, 'Practitioners must consider the individual needs, interests and stages of development of each child in their care' (DfE, 2017). It is a requirement that early years educators also liaise with parents regularly to share observations and discuss their child's needs, then any areas where they may need additional support can be identified. Planning to follow children's interests helps to encourage engagement in activities. When children are fully engaged in activities learning opportunities are enhanced.

Social learning (Bandura)

This describes how by observing/watching others, children learn new information and new ways of doing things. If you show respect and kindness to adults and children in the nursery, and at home, children will see and hear this, and they will copy what adults do.

Where do you see this theory in the EYFS?
As part of the EYFS, the Development matters guidance encourages adults to act as good role models and for example, 'Model being fair, e.g. when choosing children for special jobs' (DfE, 2012). Modelling positive behaviour and good manners is important for showing how to interact appropriately with others in a kind and respectful way.

Activity 5

Read and reflect on these two quotations. Research and write about other theorists who have also had an influence on the EYFS and *Development Matters*.

How do you plan activities for children in order that they are 'mindful of the moment', that their interests are included, and that there will be a good level of curious engagement? Give examples and details of such activities and your role within them.

Those working in Early Years acknowledge that early pioneers and theorists have influenced and contributed widely to twenty-first century Early Years theory and practice. Many of these theorists' ideas are used in current child development writings, and help to inform developmentally appropriate practice. In the above section, theorists' influence on some of the documents produced for the Early Years sector is evident. In this section more theorists are explored, and their thinking is outlined briefly in order to draw attention to how their thoughts and ideas are still relevant today. They are listed in chronological order by their birth dates.

Robert Owen (1771–1858)

- Understood the importance of a rational approach to teaching.
- He built a model community that included a day nursery and a playground in 1817.
- His biggest influence was getting children out of their workplace and into education.

Friedrich Froebel (1782–1852)

- Froebel believed 'that the kindergarten was to be an environment in which children could reach their full creative potential under the protective guidance of an adult'.
- Froebel based his system around play materials, which he called 'gifts', and activities that he called 'occupations'.

John Dewey (1859–1952)

- Dewey was a founder of a philosophical movement called pragmatism.
- He believed that a child's daily experience is critical to his/her learning and that the curriculum should relate to the lives of children.

Margaret McMillan (1860–1931)

- A great advocate of providing outdoor spaces for children to play and move with freedom.
- She believed that practitioners must look after the holistic needs of children.
- She also thought that the key development period for children was 0–6 years old and that this period of development shapes their lives.

Maria Montessori (1870–1952)

- Maria Montessori believed in the importance of the senses and in encouraging the independence of a child.
- She believed that only by developing the intellect could the imagination and social relationships emerge.
- She encouraged freedom within a structured environment.

Susan Isaacs (1885–1948)

- She encouraged staff to allow children to make sense of the world at their own pace and through their own experiences.
- Some of Susan Isaacs' ideas are now used in the modern Forest School approach.

Lev Vygotsky (1896–1934)

- Vygotsky based most of his work on thought, language and psychology, and believed that development mostly came from adults, language and the environment.
- He encouraged teachers and educators to speak to children clearly – children would then be more attentive and therefore learn more.

Jean Piaget (1896–1980)

- Many education curriculums are run on the thought that children should be taught towards their level and, if they are not ready, they will not move on.
- He focused on intellectual development and believed children develop because of their personal interactions.

Erik Erikson (1902–1994)

- Erikson believed that an individual develops on three levels at the same time – biological, social and psychological.
- His theory of development considers the impact of external factors, such as parents and society, on personality development from childhood to adulthood.

John Bowlby (1907–1990)

- Believed that a mother's love is as important for children's psychological health, as vitamins are for physical health.
- The attachment theory grew from several papers he wrote on the effects of disrupted mother/child relationships.
- Bowlby's attachment theory states that close relationships between humans are biologically necessary, and governed by primitive mechanisms shared by other mammals.
- A special relationship is needed between baby and carer.

Urie Bronfenbrenner (1917–2005)

- He insisted that child development research and theories should recognize the positive and negative effects of a child's ecological niche.

- He focused his attention on factors in families, communities, and countries that could influence children's development and learning.

Activity 6

Reflect and analyse your own practice and consider what developmental theorists influence your setting and your practice.

Analyse the impact of these child development theories on current day thinking and Early Years provision. In your opinion, which theorist(s) have the biggest impact on a child's creative development? Give your reasons for your choice.

In the ever-changing educational and social ideas of today, look back to past theorists, theories and philosophies and then apply these to present-day thinking. What conclusion do you arrive at as to which two theorists (from those listed) have influenced modern Early Years practice the most? Reflect on the reasons why you have chosen them.

Given that this list is in chronological order, which, in your opinion, would you have liked to live in and work with children? State your reasons for your choice. Six of the theorists were born in the latter half of the nineteenth century. Why do you think this was such a productive time for the theorists? Look at the way education was being run, which children benefited the most and which children did not. Research, reflect and analyse your findings.

The following quotations, summaries and information are in alphabetical order of the theorist's surname name. These quotations are all linked to child development stages. Some children's ages are omitted in order not to give too many clues to some of the questions at the end.

Ainsworth, Mary (1913–1999)

- She worked with John Bowlby.
- Based on her observations and research, she concluded that there were three main styles of attachment – secure, anxious-avoidant and anxious-resistant.
- She devised an assessment technique called the 'Strange Situation Classification' (SSC) in order to investigate how attachments might

vary between children. She studied children between the ages of . . . and . . . She observed the behaviour of the child when briefly left alone and then reunited with their mother. This research showed the effects of attachment on behaviour.

Bandura, Albert (1925–2021)

- The Bobo doll experiment was undertaken by Bandura between 1961 and 1963. The children involved with the experiment were between . . . and . . . years old. He studied children's behaviour after they watched a human adult model act aggressively towards a 'Bobo doll'. Bandura concluded 'that children learn social behaviour such as aggression through the process of observation learning and modelling – through watching the behaviour of another person. By watching the action of others, including parents and peers, children develop new skills and acquire new information.

Bowlby, John (1907–1990)

- Theory of attachment suggests that children come into the world biologically pre-programmed to form attachment with others, because this will help them survive. Babies are born with innate behaviours that help reinforce proximity with the mother or attachment figure (e.g. crying, crawling, smiling).

- A child has an innate need to attach to one main attachment figure. A child should receive the continuous care of this single most important attachment figure for approximately the . . . . years of life.

Erikson, Erik (1902–1994)

- The 'Theory of psychosocial development' occurs between birth and approximately . . . . . . years of age, and is that, 'The trust versus mistrust stage is the most important period in a person's life because it shapes our view of the world as well as our personalities'.

- Erikson found, as children enter the pre-school years, they begin the third stage of psychosocial development centred on 'initiative versus guilt'. This is a challenge to young children developing their courage and independence. Children over the age of . . . . need to try things on their own and explore their own abilities. This helps to develop ambition and direction.

Freud, Sigmund (1856–1939)

- Freud came 'to believe that childhood experiences influenced behaviour and that these played the greatest role in shaping development and personality'. According to Freud, 'these are largely set in stone by the age of . . . . years'.

Montessori, Maria (1870–1952)

- After having studied children carefully, she came to the conclusion that the first . . . . years are the most important of life.
- The development of language is part of the development of the personality, for words are 'the natural means of expressing thoughts and establishing understanding between people'.
- Maria Montessori found that, when the child begins to think and to make sense of the written language to express his rudimentary thinking, he is ready for elementary work; and this fitness is a question not of age or other incidental circumstances but of mental maturity.

Piaget, Jean (1896–1980)

- He states that 'during the first few . . . . . . of an infant's life, its manner of taking the breast, of laying its head on the pillow etc. becomes crystallized into imperative habits. This is why education must begin in the cradle'.
- Piaget's cognitive theory suggest that during the first . . . . years of life, cognition can be seen in the child's motor action towards the environment. The sensory motor intelligence was embedded not in the mind, but in the actions and movements that the child made in direct interaction with its environment. At the end of their . . . . year children begin to use mental-symbolic processes in order to adapt to their environment.
- The child of . . . . or . . . . is saturated with adult rules. His universe is dominated by the idea that things are as they ought to be, that everyone's actions conform to laws that are both physical and moral – in a word, there is a Universal Order.
- Children of . . . . . . years old are in the later stages of Piaget's 'preoperational period'. During this time, the emergence and use of language is one of the pivotal stages in the preoperational period of their development. Although their language and thinking are getting better, they think about the world around them in concrete terms.

Pringle, Mia Kellmer (1920–1983)

- She believed that needs should be met using a holistic approach rather than viewing them in a hierarchical manner, and that all needs are interrelated and interdependent. If a child is to develop to their full potential, all their social, emotional and cultural needs must be met.

Vygotsky, Lev (1896–1934)

- Vygotsky believed that language develops from social interaction, for communication purposes. He viewed language as man's greatest tool for communicating with the outside world. He emphasizes the importance of social interaction for children's cognitive development. This emphasis is on what children can do rather than what they cannot do.

- Vygotsky also believed that knowledge is not adopted by the child but is contracted by the child through interaction with a more mature or experienced peer or adult.

Activity 7

Use these quotations as a starting point. Where an age is omitted, research the age of the children that the theorist is working with or writing about. Use *Development Matters* or *Birth to 5 Matters* to help in the process. *Development Matters* 'sets out pathways of children's development in broad ages and stages. However, the actual learning of young children is not so neat and orderly. The main purpose of these pathways is therefore to help you assess each child's level of development'. Children develop in different ways, and rates of development vary from child to child. 'Although development tends to follow predictable patterns overall, each child's journey will be an individual, winding pathway, unique to that child' (*Birth to 5 Matters*).

Take two or more different ages, and then reflect on the different predicted pathways this aged child/children may follow and how you can support his/her holistic development.

The next section – (Activities 8, 9, 10, 11, 12 and 13) concentrates on Development Matters for your research into children's development. The pathways of children's development presented in broad ages and stages will help you assess each child's level of development, allowing you to make informed decisions about what a child needs to learn next. These following activities are written in adult language, not children's, for added interest, as though the child were speaking to you in the first person.

Activity 8

'I make sounds to get attention in different ways, crying, hungry or unhappy.'

'I like to babble and make sounds like "mamama", "dada", I can choose whether I play with a car or a ball.'

'I am beginning to understand words that are often used, "bye bye", "no", "all gone".'

In which of the broad age and stage groups in *Development Matters* will this child be found?

After looking in the broad age and stage groups, can you identify where the child may be in their individual stage of development?

Consider what skills and learning this child may be developing in the next year.

How can you support the learning of this child's language development? Remember that a child's learning should show consistency in a range of different contexts.

Activity 9

'I am now older, I feel more confident when taken out near to home, I enjoy exploring new places.'

'My emotions have got stronger, and I sometimes suffer from temper tantrums, or I begin to cry. I do however, often laugh.'

'I reject help – me do it – and I am growing a little more independent, my favourite word is no.'

'I am beginning to talk about my emotions.'

In which of the broad age and stage groups in *Development Matters* will this child be found?

After looking in the broad age and stage groups, can you identify where the child may be in their own development?

Consider what skills and learning this child may be developing in the next year.

How can you help and support the learning of this child's emotional development? Remember consistency and different contexts.

Activity 10

'I am active, I can go up steps or stairs and use climbing apparatus, using alternate feet.'

'I like playing musical statues, skipping, hopping and standing on one leg.'

'I get plenty of practice to develop my balance and movement by riding tricycles and scooters'.

'I enjoy a group activity with my friends, when I use the large-muscle movements to play parachute games.'

In which of the broad age and stage groups in *Development Matters* will this child be found?

After looking at the broad age and stage groups, can you identify where the child may be in their own development?

Consider what skills and learning this child may be developing in the next year.

How can you help and support the learning of this child's physical development? Remember that a child's learning should show consistency and different contexts.

Activity 11

'I can now read individual letters by saying the sounds for them.'

'I can read simple phrases and sentences made up of words with known letter–sound correspondences.'

'I am able to blend sounds into words and I can read short words made of known letter–sound correspondences.'

'I enjoy re-reading books, which gives me confidence, understanding and fluency in my reading.'

In which of the broad age and stage groups in *Development Matters* will this child be found?

After looking at the broad age and stage groups, can you identify where the child may be in their own development?

Consider what skills and learning this child may be developing in the next year.

How can you help and support the learning of this child's literacy development? Remember that a child's learning should show consistency and different contexts.

Research and analyse steps in learning to read through phonics.

Outline activities that promote speaking and listening skills, phonological awareness and blending and segmenting.

Activity 12

'I enjoy activities where I can explore and express artistic effects to express my ideas and feelings.'

'I join in with other children and work together sharing ideas, resources and skills.'

'When I and my friends are "pretend playing", we make up storylines.'

'One part of the school day I enjoy taking part in is music making and dance. We sometimes perform in a group or solo.'

In which of the broad age and stage groups in *Development Matters* will this child be found?

After looking at the broad age and stage groups, can you identify where the child may be in their own development?

Consider what skills and learning this child may be developing in the next year.

How can you help and support the learning of this child's expressive arts and design development? Remember that a child's learning should show consistency and different contexts.

Research what regular opportunities you can give children of this age in order to enable them to engage with the arts. Look at ideas of exploring with different mediums and materials.

Activity 13

'I can recite numbers past five, I can show "finger numbers" up to five.'

'I can link numerals and amounts, showing the correct number of objects to match the numeral 5.'

'I can compare objects relating to size, weight, length and capacity.'

'I enjoy looking at patterns in the environment – stripes on clothes, wallpaper patterns – I can correct an error in repeating patterns.'

In which of the broad age and stage groups in *Development Matters* will this child be found?

After looking at the broad age and stage groups, can you identify where the child may be in their own development?

Consider what learning skills this child may be developing in the next year.

Research how children learn to count objects, the cardinal counting principle, how they compare numbers, and how stories, rhymes and songs can help with mathematical development.

Describe activities that will help children to have a deeper understanding of numbers up to ten, that help to develop a good vocabulary of mathematical language, and that help children have a lasting interest in mathematics.

Note: Throughout this chapter there have been many references to well-known theorists and developmentalists. It is not the intention of the writers to list them, but their areas of work are all described in the volumes noted in the Bibliography.

Bibliography and References

Ainsworth, M. and Blehar, M., Waters, E., Wall, S. *Patterns of Attachment: A Psychological Study of the Strange Situation.* London: Psychology Press, Routledge, 1979.

Arnold, A. and Rutter, R. *Working with Parents: Key Issues.* London: Featherstone Education, 2011.

Arnold, C. *Understanding Schemas and Emotion in Early Childhood.* London: Sage, 2012.

Asquith, S. *Self-Regulation Skills in Young Children: Activities and Strategies for Practitioners and Parents.* London: Jessica Kingsley Publishers, 2020.

Aubrey, K. and Riley, A. *Understanding and Using Educational Theories.* London: Sage, 2019.

Bandura, A. *Social Learning Theory.* Englewood Cliffs, NJ: Prentice Hall, 1977.

Bates, B. *Learning Theories Simplified.* London: Sage, 2015.

Bayley, R. *Child Initiated Learning: Hundreds of Ideas for Independent Learning in the Early Years.* Lutterworth: Featherstone Education, 2013.

Berryman, J., Hargreaves, D. J., Howells, K. and Ockleford, E. *Developmental Psychology and You* (3rd edn.). Oxford: Blackwell, 2006.

Bilton, H. *Outdoor Play in the Early Years: Management and Innovation* (3rd edn.). Oxford: Routledge, 2010.

Bowlby, J. *Separation: Anxiety and Anger.* London: Pimlico, 1998.

Bowlby, J. *Attachment and Loss, vol. 1* (revised edn.). London: Pimlico, 1998.

British Association for Early Childhood Education. *Development Matters in the Early Years Foundation Stage.* London: Early Education, 2012.

Brodie, K. *Observation, Assessment and Planning in the Early Years.* Milton Keynes: Open University Press, 2013.

Bronfenbrenner, U. *Making Human Beings Human.* Thousand Oaks, CA: Sage, 2005.

Bruce, T. and Meggitt, C. *Child Care and Education* (5th edn.). London: Hodder, 2010.

Bruner, J. *Actual Minds, Possible Worlds.* Cambridge, MA: Harvard College, 1986.

Carr, M. *Assessment in Early Childhood Settings: Learning Stories.* London: Sage, 2001.

Clark, A. and Moss, P. *Listening to Young Children: The Mosaic Approach.* London: NCB, 2001.

Conkbayir, M. and Pascal, C. *Early Childhood Theories and Contemporary Issues: An Introduction.* London: Bloomsbury, 2015.

Constable, K. *Bringing the Forest School Approach to your Early Years Practice.* New York: Routledge, 2014.

Dale-Tunnicliffe, S. *Talking and Doing Science in the Early Years; A Practical Guide for Ages 2 to 7.* Oxford: Routledge, 2013.

Daly, L. and Beloglovsky, M. *Loose Parts: Inspiring Play in Young Children.* St. Paul, MN: Red Leaf Press, 2014.

Daly, L. and Beloglovsky, M. *Loose Parts 3: Inspiring Culturally Sustainable Environments.* St. Paul. MN: Red Leaf Press, 2018.

Dewey, J. *Experience and Education.* London: Free Press, Simon and Schuster, 2008.

DfE. (Department for Education). *2014 EYFS Profile – Handbook.* London: DfE, 2014.

DfE. (Department for Education). *Statutory Framework for the Early Years Foundation Stage: Setting the Standards for Learning, Development and Care for Children from Birth to Five.* London: DfE, 2017.

DfE. (Department for Education). *Development Matters.* London: DfE, September 2020.

DfE. (Department for Education). *EYFS Framework Early Adopter Handbook.* London: DfE, 2020.

DfE. (Department for Education). *Early Years Foundation Stage Profile.* London: DfE, 2020.

DfE. (2020). *Statutory Framework for The Early Years Foundation Stage. EYFS Reforms Early Adopter Version.* London: DfE, July 2020.

DfE. (Department for Education). *Statutory Framework for the Early Years Foundation Stage.* London: DfE, 2021.

Donnachie, I. *Robert Owen – Social Visionary.* Edinburgh, Scotland: John Donald Publishers, 2005.

Drummond, M. Observing children. In S. Smidt (ed.), *The Early Years: A Reader.* London and New York: Routledge, 1998.

EE (Early Education). *Development Matters in the Early Years Foundation Stage (EYFS).* London. Early Education, 2020.

Early Years Coalition, *Birth to 5 Matters.* St. Albans: Early Education, 2021.

Early Years Foundation Stage. *Effective Practice: Outdoor Learning.* Available at: http://outdoormatters.co.uk/wp-content/uploads/2011/03/EYFS-Effective-PracticeOutdoor-Learning.pdf, 2007.

Early Years Guidance, Theories of development: How they have influenced the EYFS, 5 January 2020. Available at: https://earlyyearseducatorguidance.wordpress.com/2020/01/05/theories-of-development-how-they-have-influenced-the-eyfs/

Elfer, P., Abbott, L. and Langston, A. (eds), *Birth to Three Matters.* Maidenhead: Open University Press, 2005.

Ephgrave, A. *Planning in the Moment with Young Children: A Practical Guide for Early Years Practitioners and Parents.* London: Routledge, 2018.

Erikson, E.H. *Childhood and Society* (2nd edn.). New York: Norton, 1963.

Fishbein, H. *The Psychology of Infancy and Childhood: Evolutionary and Cross Cultural Perspectives.* Hillsdale NJ: Erlbaum, 1984.

Flensburg-Maden, T. and Mortensen, E. L. Predictors of motor developmental milestones during first year of life. *European Journal of Pediatrics*, 176(1), 109–19, 2017 January.

Geraghty, P. *Caring for Children* (2dn edn.). London: Bailliere Tindall, 1988.

Gesell, A. *The First Five Years of Life.* London: Methuen, 1950.

Giardiello, P. *Pioneers in Early Childhood, The Roots and Legacies of Rachel and Margaret McMillan, Maria Montessori and Susan Isaacs.* London: Routledge, 2013.

Goleman, D. *Working with Emotional Intelligence.* London: Bloomsbury, 1999.

Gray, C. and MacBlain, S. *Learning Theories in Childhood* (2nd edn.). London: Sage, 2015.

Green, S. *Research Methods in Early Years.* Cheltenham, UK: Nelson Thorne, 2002.

Grieve, R. and Hughes, M. (eds.) *Understanding Children.* Oxford: Blackwell, 1990.

Hadland, C. *Creating an Eco-Friendly Early Years Setting – A Practical Guide.* London: Routledge, 2020.

Hall, K. Cunneen, M. Murphy, R. *Loris Malaguzzi and the Reggio Emilia Experience.* London: Continuum, 2010.

Hellyn, L. and Bennett, S. *The A to Z of the Curiosity Approach.* Birmingham: The Curiosity Approach, 2017.

House, R. *Too Much, Too Soon? Early Learning and the Erosion of Childhood.* Stroud: Hawthorn Press, 2011.

Inhelder, B., and Piaget, J. *The Growth of Logical Thinking from Childhood to Adolescence.* New York: Basic Books, 1958.

Isaacs, B. *Understanding the Montessori Approach.* Oxford: Routledge, 2012.

Isaacs, S. *The Nursery Years: The Mind of the Child from Birth to Six Years.* London. Routledge, 1929.

Katz, L. G. A developmental approach to the curriculum in the Early Years. In S. Smidt (ed.), *The Early Years: A Reader.* London: Routledge, 1998.

Kellmer Pringle, M. *The Needs of Children* (3rd edn.). London: Routledge, 1990.

Knight, S. *Forest School and Outdoor Learning in the Early Years* (2nd edn.). London: Sage, 2013.

Leman, P. and Bremner, A. *Developmental Psychology* (2nd edn.). Europe, McGraw Hill Education, 2020.

Lindon, J. *Reflective Practice and Early Years Professionalism* (2nd edn.). London: Hodder, 2012.

Luff, P. *Written Observations or Walks in the Park: Documenting Children's Experiences in Early Years Foundations: Meeting the Challenge.* Maidenhead: Open University Press, 2007.

Macleod-Brudenell, I., Kay, J. and Cortvriend, V. *Advanced Early Years; For Foundation Degrees & Level 4/5* (2nd edn.), Oxford: Heinemann, 2008.

Maslow, A. *Hierarchy of Needs: A Theory of Human Motivation.* London: all-about-psychology.com, 2011.

McLeod, S.A. Jean Piaget's theory of cognitive development. *Simply Psychology.* www.simplypsychology.org/piaget.html (2018, 6 June).

McMillan, M. *The Nursery School.* Charleston, S. Carolina: BiblioLife, 2009.

Montague-Smith, A. and Price, A.J. *Mathematics in Early Years Education.* London: Routledge, 2012.

Montessori, M. *The Absorbent Mind.* New York: BN Publishing, 2009.

Montessori, M. *The Montessori Method.* New York: Frederick A. Stokes Company, 1912.

Moomaw, S. *Teaching Stem in the Early Years: Activities for Integrating Science, Technology, Engineering and Mathematics.* St. Paul, MN: Red Leaf Press, 2013.

Moyles, J. *The Excellence of Play* (3rd edn.). Maidenhead: Open University Press, 2010.

Moyles, J. and Papatheodorou, T. *Learning Together in the Early Years: Exploring Relational Pedagogy.* London: Routledge, 2009.

Neaum, S. *Language and Literacy for the Early Years.* London: Sage, 2012.

Ott, P. *How to Detect and Manage Dyslexia.* London: Heinemann, 1997.

Paige-Smith, A. and Craft, A. (eds), *Developing Reflective Practice in the Early Years.* Maidenhead: Open University Press, 2007.

Palaiologou, I. *Ethical Practice in Early Childhood.* London: Sage, 2012.

Palaiologou, I. *The Early Years Foundation Stage Theory and Practice* (2nd edn.). London: Sage, 2013.

Palaiologou, I. *Child Observation for the Early Years* (3rd edn.). London: Sage, 2016.

Papatheodorou, T., Luff, P. and Gill, J. *Child Observation for Learning and Research.* London: Pearson, 2011.

Piaget, J. *The Child's Conception of the World.* New York: Harcourt Brace, 1929.

Powell, S., Gooch, K., and David, T. *International Handbook of Philosophies and Theories of Early Childhood Education and Care.* London: Routledge, 2015.

Rinaldi, C. *The Hundred Languages of Children: The Reggio Emilia Approach to Early Childhood Education.* New York: Ablex Publishing, 1995.

Saltman, B. *Strange Situation: A Mother's Journey into the Science of Attachment.* New York: Ballantine Books, 2020.

Scheck, S. *The Stages of Psychosocial Development According to Erik H. Erikson.* Germany: GRIN Verlag, 2014.

Sheridan, M. *From Birth to Five Years* (3rd edn.). London: NFER, 2003.

Skinner, B.F. *About Behaviourism.* New York: Vintage Edition Books, 1976.

Smidt, S. *Observing, Assessing and Planning for Children in the Early Years.* London: Routledge, 2005.

Smith, K. *Hugge in The Early Years.* Independently published, 2017.

Stanford Children's Health (n.d.). Your Child's Social and Emotional Development, www.stanfordchildrens.org

Stoll Lillard, A. *Montessori: The Science behind the Genius* (updated edition). New York: Oxford University Press, 2008.

Sutherland, H. and Maxey, A. In J. Johnson (ed.), *Becoming an Early Years Teacher.* Milton Keynes: Open University Press, 2014.

Sylva, K., Melhuish, E. Sammons, P., Siraj-Blatchford, I. and Taggart, B. *Early Childhood Matters.* Oxford: Routledge, 2010.

Tough, J. *Listening to Children Talking.* London: Ward Lock Education, 1976.

Trodd, L. *The Early Years Handbook for Students and Practitioners: An Essential Guide for the Foundation Degree Levels 4 and 5.* Abingdon: Oxon, 2016.

UNICEF. *The United Nations Convention on the Rights of the Child* (UNCRC). London: UNICEF, 1989.

Vygotsky, L. *Thought and Language* (2nd edn.). Cambridge, MA: The MIT Press, 1986.

Vygotsky, L.S. *Mind and Society: The Development of Higher Mental Processes,* Cambridge MA: Harvard University Press, 1978.

Weston, P. *Friedrich Froebel: His Life, His Times and Significance.* London: University of Surrey, Roehampton, 2000.

White, J. *Making a Mud Kitchen* (2nd edn.). Sheffield: Muddy Faces, 2018.

Winnicott, D.W. *The Child, the Family, and the Outside World.* New York: Addison-Wesley Publishing Company, 1987.

Wood, E. *Play, Learning and the Early Childhood Curriculum.* London. Sage, 2013.

Woolfson, R. See the funny side – virtual sense of humour, *Nursery World,* 16 February 2000. Available at: https://www.nurseryworld.co.uk/News/article/see-the-funny-side-virtual-sense-of-humour

Index

www.ingramcontent.com/pod-product-compliance
Ingram Content Group UK Ltd.
Pitfield, Milton Keynes, MK11 3LW, UK
UKHW020729020325
455688UK00015B/213